GNU libmicrohttpd Reference Manual

A catalogue record for this book is available from the Hong Kong Public Libraries.

Published in Hong Kong by Samurai Media Limited.

Email: info@samuraimedia.org

ISBN 978-988-8381-55-5

Short Contents

Table of Contents

1 Introduction

All symbols defined in the public API start with `MHD_`. MHD is a small HTTP daemon library. As such, it does not have any API for logging errors (you can only enable or disable logging to stderr). Also, it may not support all of the HTTP features directly, where applicable, portions of HTTP may have to be handled by clients of the library.

The library is supposed to handle everything that it must handle (because the API would not allow clients to do this), such as basic connection management; however, detailed interpretations of headers — such as range requests — and HTTP methods are left to clients. The library does understand `HEAD` and will only send the headers of the response and not the body, even if the client supplied a body. The library also understands headers that control connection management (specifically, `Connection: close` and `Expect: 100 continue` are understood and handled automatically).

MHD understands `POST` data and is able to decode certain formats (at the moment only `application/x-www-form-urlencoded` and `multipart/form-data`) using the post processor API. The data stream of a POST is also provided directly to the main application, so unsupported encodings could still be processed, just not conveniently by MHD.

The header file defines various constants used by the HTTP protocol. This does not mean that MHD actually interprets all of these values. The provided constants are exported as a convenience for users of the library. MHD does not verify that transmitted HTTP headers are part of the standard specification; users of the library are free to define their own extensions of the HTTP standard and use those with MHD.

All functions are guaranteed to be completely reentrant and thread-safe. MHD checks for allocation failures and tries to recover gracefully (for example, by closing the connection). Additionally, clients can specify resource limits on the overall number of connections, number of connections per IP address and memory used per connection to avoid resource exhaustion.

1.1 Scope

MHD is currently used in a wide range of implementations. Examples based on reports we've received from developers include:

- Embedded HTTP server on a cortex M3 (128 KB code space)
- Large-scale multimedia server (reportedly serving at the simulator limit of 7.5 GB/s)
- Administrative console (via HTTP/HTTPS) for network appliances

1.2 Thread modes and event loops

MHD supports four basic thread modes and up to three event loop styes.

The four basic thread modes are external (MHD creates no threads, event loop is fully managed by the application), internal (MHD creates one thread for all connections), thread pool (MHD creates a thread pool which is used to process all connections) and thread-per-connection (MHD creates one listen thread and then one thread per accepted connection).

These thread modes are then combined with the event loop styles. MHD support select, poll and epoll. epoll is only available on Linux, poll may not be available on some platforms.

Note that it is possible to combine MHD using epoll with an external select-based event loop.

The default (if no other option is passed) is "external select". The highest performance can typically be obtained with a thread pool using **epoll**. Apache Benchmark (ab) was used to compare the performance of **select** and **epoll** when using a thread pool and a large number of connections. Figure 1.1 shows the resulting plot from the **benchmark.c** example, which measures the latency between an incoming request and the completion of the transmission of the response. In this setting, the **epoll** thread pool with four threads was able to handle more than 45,000 connections per second on loopback (with Apache Benchmark running three processes on the same machine).

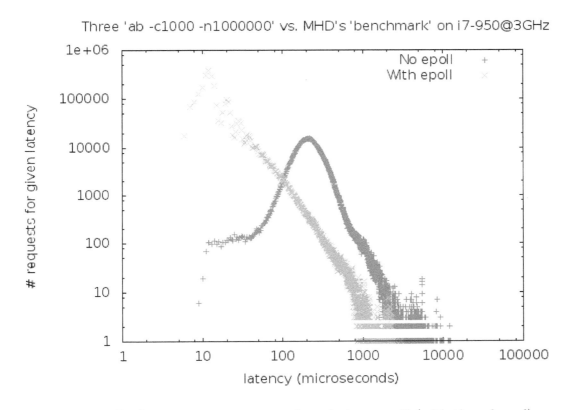

Figure 1.1: Performance measurements for select vs. epoll (with thread-pool).

Not all combinations of thread modes and event loop styles are supported. This is partially to keep the API simple, and partially because some combinations simply make no sense as others are strictly superior. Note that the choice of style depends fist of all on the application logic, and then on the performance requirements. Applications that perform a blocking operation while handling a request within the callbacks from MHD must use a thread per connection. This is typically rather costly. Applications that do not support threads or that must run on embedded devices without thread-support must use the external mode. Using **epoll** is only supported on Linux, thus portable applications must at least have a fallback option available. Table 1.1 lists the sane combinations.

	select	poll	epoll
external	yes	no	yes
internal	yes	yes	yes
thread pool	yes	yes	yes
thread-per-connection	yes	yes	no

Table 1.1: Supported combinations of event styles and thread modes.

1.3 Compiling GNU libmicrohttpd

MHD uses the standard GNU system where the usual build process involves running

```
$ ./configure
$ make
$ make install
```

MHD supports various options to be given to configure to tailor the binary to a specific situation. Note that some of these options will remove portions of the MHD code that are required for binary-compatibility. They should only be used on embedded systems with tight resource constraints and no concerns about library versioning. Standard distributions including MHD are expected to always ship with all features enabled, otherwise unexpected incompatibilities can arise!

Here is a list of MHD-specific options that can be given to configure (canonical configure options such as "–prefix" are also supported, for a full list of options run "./configure –help"):

``--disable-curl``
> disable running testcases using libcurl

``--disable-largefile``
> disable support for 64-bit files

``--disable-messages``
> disable logging of error messages (smaller binary size, not so much fun for debugging)

``--disable-https``
> disable HTTPS support, even if GNUtls is found; this option must be used if eCOS license is desired as an option (in all cases the resulting binary falls under a GNU LGPL-only license)

``--disable-postprocessor``
> do not include the post processor API (results in binary incompatibility)

``--disable-dauth``
> do not include the authentication APIs (results in binary incompatibility)

``--disable-epoll``
> do not include epoll support, even on Linux (minimally smaller binary size, good for testing portability to non-Linux systems)

``--enable-coverage``
> set flags for analysis of code-coverage with gcc/gcov (results in slow, large binaries)

`` `--with-gcrypt=PATH' ``
>   specifies path to libgcrypt installation

`` `--with-gnutls=PATH' ``
>   specifies path to libgnutls installation

1.4 Including the microhttpd.h header

Ideally, before including "microhttpd.h" you should add the necessary includes to define the `uint64_t`, `size_t`, `fd_set`, `socklen_t` and `struct sockaddr` data types. Which specific headers are needed may depend on your platform and your build system might include some tests to provide you with the necessary conditional operations. For possible suggestions consult `platform.h` and `configure.ac` in the MHD distribution.

Once you have ensured that you manually (!) included the right headers for your platform before "microhttpd.h", you should also add a line with `#define MHD_PLATFORM_H` which will prevent the "microhttpd.h" header from trying (and, depending on your platform, failing) to include the right headers.

If you do not define MHD_PLATFORM_H, the "microhttpd.h" header will automatically include headers needed on GNU/Linux systems (possibly causing problems when porting to other platforms).

1.5 SIGPIPE

MHD does not install a signal handler for SIGPIPE. On platforms where this is possible (such as GNU/Linux), it disables SIGPIPE for its I/O operations (by passing MSG_NOSIGNAL). On other platforms, SIGPIPE signals may be generated from network operations by MHD and will cause the process to die unless the developer explicitly installs a signal handler for SIGPIPE.

Hence portable code using MHD must install a SIGPIPE handler or explicitly block the SIGPIPE signal. MHD does not do so in order to avoid messing with other parts of the application that may need to handle SIGPIPE in a particular way. You can make your application handle SIGPIPE by calling the following function in **main**:

```
static void
catcher (int sig)
{
}

static void
ignore_sigpipe ()
{
  struct sigaction oldsig;
  struct sigaction sig;

  sig.sa_handler = &catcher;
  sigemptyset (&sig.sa_mask);
#ifdef SA_INTERRUPT
  sig.sa_flags = SA_INTERRUPT;   /* SunOS */
```

```
#else
  sig.sa_flags = SA_RESTART;
#endif
  if (0 != sigaction (SIGPIPE, &sig, &oldsig))
    fprintf (stderr,
              "Failed to install SIGPIPE handler: %s\n", strerror (errno));
}
```

1.6 MHD_UNSIGNED_LONG_LONG

Some platforms do not support `long long`. Hence MHD defines a macro `MHD_UNSIGNED LONG_LONG` which will default to `unsigned long long`. For standard desktop operating systems, this is all you need to know.

However, if your platform does not support `unsigned long long`, you should change "platform.h" to define `MHD_LONG_LONG` and `MHD_UNSIGNED_LONG_LONG` to an appropriate alternative type and also define `MHD_LONG_LONG_PRINTF` and `MHD_UNSIGNED_LONG_LONG_PRINTF` to the corresponding format string for printing such a data type. Note that the "signed" versions are deprecated. Also, for historical reasons, `MHD_LONG_LONG_PRINTF` is without the percent sign, whereas `MHD_UNSIGNED_LONG_LONG_PRINTF` is with the percent sign. Newly written code should only use the unsigned versions. However, you need to define both in "platform.h" if you need to change the definition for the specific platform.

1.7 Portability to W32

libmicrohttpd in general ported well to W32. Most libmicrohttpd features are supported. W32 do not support some functions, like epoll and corresponding MHD features are not available on W32.

1.8 Portability to z/OS

To compile MHD on z/OS, extract the archive and run

```
iconv -f UTF-8 -t IBM-1047 contrib/ascebc > /tmp/ascebc.sh
chmod +x /tmp/ascebc.sh
for n in 'find * -type f'
do
  /tmp/ascebc.sh $n
done
```

to convert all source files to EBCDIC. Note that you must run `configure` from the directory where the configure script is located. Otherwise, configure will fail to find the `contrib/xcc` script (which is a wrapper around the z/OS c89 compiler).

2 Constants

`MHD_FLAG`   [Enumeration]

Options for the MHD daemon.

Note that if neither `MHD_USE_THREAD_PER_CONNECTION` nor `MHD_USE_SELECT_ INTERNALLY` is used, the client wants control over the process and will call the appropriate microhttpd callbacks.

Starting the daemon may also fail if a particular option is not implemented or not supported on the target platform (i.e. no support for SSL, threads or IPv6). SSL support generally depends on options given during MHD compilation. Threaded operations (including `MHD_USE_SELECT_INTERNALLY`) are not supported on Symbian.

`MHD_NO_FLAG`

No options selected.

`MHD_USE_DEBUG`

Run in debug mode. If this flag is used, the library should print error messages and warnings to stderr. Note that for this run-time option to have any effect, MHD needs to be compiled with messages enabled. This is done by default except you ran configure with the `--disable-messages` flag set.

`MHD_USE_SSL`

Run in HTTPS-mode. If you specify `MHD_USE_SSL` and MHD was compiled without SSL support, `MHD_start_daemon` will return NULL.

`MHD_USE_THREAD_PER_CONNECTION`

Run using one thread per connection.

`MHD_USE_SELECT_INTERNALLY`

Run using an internal thread doing `SELECT`.

`MHD_USE_IPv6`

Run using the IPv6 protocol (otherwise, MHD will just support IPv4). If you specify `MHD_USE_IPV6` and the local platform does not support it, `MHD_start_daemon` will return NULL.

If you want MHD to support IPv4 and IPv6 using a single socket, pass MHD_USE_DUAL_STACK, otherwise, if you only pass this option, MHD will try to bind to IPv6-only (resulting in no IPv4 support).

`MHD_USE_DUAL_STACK`

Use a single socket for IPv4 and IPv6. Note that this will mean that IPv4 addresses are returned by MHD in the IPv6-mapped format (the 'struct sockaddr_in6' format will be used for IPv4 and IPv6).

`MHD_USE_PEDANTIC_CHECKS`

Be pedantic about the protocol (as opposed to as tolerant as possible). Specifically, at the moment, this flag causes MHD to reject HTTP 1.1 connections without a `Host` header. This is required by the standard, but of course in violation of the "be as liberal as possible in what you accept" norm. It is recommended to turn this **ON** if you are testing clients against MHD, and **OFF** in production.

MHD_USE_POLL

Use poll instead of select. This allows sockets with descriptors `>= FD_SETSIZE`. This option currently only works in conjunction with `MHD_USE_THREAD_PER_CONNECTION` or `MHD_USE_INTERNAL_SELECT` (at this point). If you specify `MHD_USE_POLL` and the local platform does not support it, `MHD_start_daemon` will return NULL.

MHD_USE_EPOLL_LINUX_ONLY

Use epoll instead of poll or select. This allows sockets with descriptors `>= FD_SETSIZE`. This option is only available on Linux systems and only works in conjunction with `MHD_USE_THREAD_PER_CONNECTION` (at this point). If you specify `MHD_USE_EPOLL_LINUX_ONLY` and the local platform does not support it, `MHD_start_daemon` will return NULL. Using epoll instead of select or poll can in some situations result in significantly higher performance as the system call has fundamentally lower complexity (O(1) for epoll vs. O(n) for select/poll where n is the number of open connections).

MHD_SUPPRESS_DATE_NO_CLOCK

Suppress (automatically) adding the 'Date:' header to HTTP responses. This option should ONLY be used on systems that do not have a clock and that DO provide other mechanisms for cache control. See also RFC 2616, section 14.18 (exception 3).

MHD_USE_NO_LISTEN_SOCKET

Run the HTTP server without any listen socket. This option only makes sense if `MHD_add_connection` is going to be used exclusively to connect HTTP clients to the HTTP server. This option is incompatible with using a thread pool; if it is used, `MHD_OPTION_THREAD_POOL_SIZE` is ignored.

MHD_USE_PIPE_FOR_SHUTDOWN

Force MHD to use a signal pipe to notify the event loop (of threads) of our shutdown. This is required if an appliction uses `MHD_USE_INTERNAL_SELECT` or `MHD_USE_THREAD_PER_CONNECTION` and then performs `MHD_quiesce_daemon` (which eliminates our ability to signal termination via the listen socket). In these modes, `MHD_quiesce_daemon` will fail if this option was not set. Also, use of this option is automatic (as in, you do not even have to specify it), if `MHD_USE_NO_LISTEN_SOCKET` is specified. In "external" select mode, this option is always simply ignored.

MHD_USE_SUSPEND_RESUME

Enables using `MHD_suspend_connection` and `MHD_resume_connection`, as performing these calls requires some additional pipes to be created, and code not using these calls should not pay the cost.

MHD_USE_TCP_FASTOPEN

> Enable TCP_FASTOPEN on the listen socket. TCP_FASTOPEN is currently supported on Linux >= 3.6. On other systems using this option with cause `MHD_start_daemon` to fail.

`MHD_OPTION`   [Enumeration]

MHD options. Passed in the varargs portion of `MHD_start_daemon()`.

MHD_OPTION_END

> No more options / last option. This is used to terminate the VARARGs list.

MHD_OPTION_CONNECTION_MEMORY_LIMIT

> Maximum memory size per connection (followed by a `size_t`). The default is 32 kB (32*1024 bytes) as defined by the internal constant `MHD_POOL_SIZE_DEFAULT`. Values above 128k are unlikely to result in much benefit, as half of the memory will be typically used for IO, and TCP buffers are unlikely to support window sizes above 64k on most systems.

MHD_OPTION_CONNECTION_MEMORY_INCREMENT

> Increment to use for growing the read buffer (followed by a `size_t`). The default is 1024 (bytes). Increasing this value will make MHD use memory for reading more aggressively, which can reduce the number of `recvfrom` calls but may increase the number of `sendto` calls. The given value must fit within MHD_OPTION_CONNECTION_MEMORY_LIMIT.

MHD_OPTION_CONNECTION_LIMIT

> Maximum number of concurrent connections to accept (followed by an `unsigned int`). The default is `FD_SETSIZE - 4` (the maximum number of file descriptors supported by `select` minus four for `stdin`, `stdout`, `stderr` and the server socket). In other words, the default is as large as possible.
>
> Note that if you set a low connection limit, you can easily get into trouble with browsers doing request pipelining. For example, if your connection limit is "1", a browser may open a first connection to access your "index.html" file, keep it open but use a second connection to retrieve CSS files, images and the like. In fact, modern browsers are typically by default configured for up to 15 parallel connections to a single server. If this happens, MHD will refuse to even accept the second connection until the first connection is closed — which does not happen until timeout. As a result, the browser will fail to render the page and seem to hang. If you expect your server to operate close to the connection limit, you should first consider using a lower timeout value and also possibly add a "Connection: close" header to your response to ensure that request pipelining is not used and connections are closed immediately after the request has completed:

```
MHD_add_response_header (response,
                        MHD_HTTP_HEADER_CONNECTION,
                        "close");
```

MHD_OPTION_CONNECTION_TIMEOUT

> After how many seconds of inactivity should a connection automatically be timed out? (followed by an **unsigned int**; use zero for no timeout). The default is zero (no timeout).

MHD_OPTION_NOTIFY_COMPLETED

> Register a function that should be called whenever a request has been completed (this can be used for application-specific clean up). Requests that have never been presented to the application (via **MHD_AccessHandlerCallback()**) will not result in notifications.

> This option should be followed by **TWO** pointers. First a pointer to a function of type **MHD_RequestCompletedCallback()** and second a pointer to a closure to pass to the request completed callback. The second pointer maybe **NULL**.

MHD_OPTION_PER_IP_CONNECTION_LIMIT

> Limit on the number of (concurrent) connections made to the server from the same IP address. Can be used to prevent one IP from taking over all of the allowed connections. If the same IP tries to establish more than the specified number of connections, they will be immediately rejected. The option should be followed by an **unsigned int**. The default is zero, which means no limit on the number of connections from the same IP address.

MHD_OPTION_SOCK_ADDR

> Bind daemon to the supplied socket address. This option should be followed by a **struct sockaddr ***. If **MHD_USE_IPv6** is specified, the **struct sockaddr*** should point to a **struct sockaddr_in6**, otherwise to a **struct sockaddr_in**. If this option is not specified, the daemon will listen to incoming connections from anywhere. If you use this option, the 'port' argument from **MHD_start_daemon** is ignored and the port from the given **struct sockaddr *** will be used instead.

MHD_OPTION_URI_LOG_CALLBACK

> Specify a function that should be called before parsing the URI from the client. The specified callback function can be used for processing the URI (including the options) before it is parsed. The URI after parsing will no longer contain the options, which maybe inconvenient for logging. This option should be followed by two arguments, the first one must be of the form

> > void * my_logger(void * cls, const char * uri, struct MHD_Connecti

> where the return value will be passed as ***con_cls** in calls to the **MHD_AccessHandlerCallback** when this request is processed later; returning a value of **NULL** has no special significance; (however, note that if you return non-**NULL**, you can no longer rely on the first call to the access handler having **NULL == *con_cls** on entry) **cls** will be set to the second argument following MHD_OPTION_URI_LOG_CALLBACK. Finally, **uri** will be the 0-terminated URI of the request.

Note that during the time of this call, most of the connection's state is not initialized (as we have not yet parsed he headers). However, information about the connecting client (IP, socket) is available.

MHD_OPTION_HTTPS_MEM_KEY

Memory pointer to the private key to be used by the HTTPS daemon. This option should be followed by an "const char*" argument. This should be used in conjunction with 'MHD_OPTION_HTTPS_MEM_CERT'.

MHD_OPTION_HTTPS_MEM_CERT

Memory pointer to the certificate to be used by the HTTPS daemon. This option should be followed by an "const char*" argument. This should be used in conjunction with 'MHD_OPTION_HTTPS_MEM_KEY'.

MHD_OPTION_HTTPS_MEM_TRUST

Memory pointer to the CA certificate to be used by the HTTPS daemon to authenticate and trust clients certificates. This option should be followed by an "const char*" argument. The presence of this option activates the request of certificate to the client. The request to the client is marked optional, and it is the responsibility of the server to check the presence of the certificate if needed. Note that most browsers will only present a client certificate only if they have one matching the specified CA, not sending any certificate otherwise.

MHD_OPTION_HTTPS_CRED_TYPE

Daemon credentials type. Either certificate or anonymous, this option should be followed by one of the values listed in "enum gnutls_credentials_type_t".

MHD_OPTION_HTTPS_PRIORITIES

SSL/TLS protocol version and ciphers. This option must be followed by an "const char *" argument specifying the SSL/TLS protocol versions and ciphers that are acceptable for the application. The string is passed unchanged to gnutls_priority_init. If this option is not specified, "NORMAL" is used.

MHD_OPTION_HTTPS_CERT_CALLBACK

Use a callback to determine which X.509 certificate should be used for a given HTTPS connection. This option should be followed by a argument of type "gnutls_certificate_retrieve_function2 *". This option provides an alternative to MHD_OPTION_HTTPS_MEM_KEY and MHD_OPTION_HTTPS_MEM_CERT. You must use this version if multiple domains are to be hosted at the same IP address using TLS's Server Name Indication (SNI) extension. In this case, the callback is expected to select the correct certificate based on the SNI information provided. The callback is expected to access the SNI data using gnutls_server_name_get(). Using this option requires GnuTLS 3.0 or higher.

MHD_OPTION_DIGEST_AUTH_RANDOM

> Digest Authentication nonce's seed.
>
> This option should be followed by two arguments. First an integer of type "size_t" which specifies the size of the buffer pointed to by the second argument in bytes. Note that the application must ensure that the buffer of the second argument remains allocated and unmodified while the daemon is running. For security, you SHOULD provide a fresh random nonce when using MHD with Digest Authentication.

MHD_OPTION_NONCE_NC_SIZE

> Size of an array of nonce and nonce counter map. This option must be followed by an "unsigned int" argument that have the size (number of elements) of a map of a nonce and a nonce-counter. If this option is not specified, a default value of 4 will be used (which might be too small for servers handling many requests). If you do not use digest authentication at all, you can specify a value of zero to save some memory.
>
> You should calculate the value of NC_SIZE based on the number of connections per second multiplied by your expected session duration plus a factor of about two for hash table collisions. For example, if you expect 100 digest-authenticated connections per second and the average user to stay on your site for 5 minutes, then you likely need a value of about 60000. On the other hand, if you can only expect only 10 digest-authenticated connections per second, tolerate browsers getting a fresh nonce for each request and expect a HTTP request latency of 250 ms, then a value of about 5 should be fine.

MHD_OPTION_LISTEN_SOCKET

> Listen socket to use. Pass a listen socket for MHD to use (systemd-style). If this option is used, MHD will not open its own listen socket(s). The argument passed must be of type "int" and refer to an existing socket that has been bound to a port and is listening.

MHD_OPTION_EXTERNAL_LOGGER

> Use the given function for logging error messages. This option must be followed by two arguments; the first must be a pointer to a function of type 'void fun(void * arg, const char * fmt, va_list ap)' and the second a pointer of type 'void*' which will be passed as the "arg" argument to "fun".
>
> Note that MHD will not generate any log messages without the MHD_USE_DEBUG flag set and if MHD was compiled with the "–disable-messages" flag.

MHD_OPTION_THREAD_POOL_SIZE

> Number (unsigned int) of threads in thread pool. Enable thread pooling by setting this value to to something greater than 1. Currently, thread model must be MHD_USE_SELECT_INTERNALLY if thread pooling is enabled (MHD_start_daemon returns NULL for an unsupported thread model).

MHD_OPTION_ARRAY

> This option can be used for initializing MHD using options from an array. A common use for this is writing an FFI for MHD. The actual options given are in an array of 'struct MHD_OptionItem', so this option requires a single argument of type 'struct MHD_OptionItem'. The array must be terminated with an entry `MHD_OPTION_END`.
>
> An example for code using MHD_OPTION_ARRAY is:

```
struct MHD_OptionItem ops[] = {
  { MHD_OPTION_CONNECTION_LIMIT, 100, NULL },
  { MHD_OPTION_CONNECTION_TIMEOUT, 10, NULL },
  { MHD_OPTION_END, 0, NULL }
};
d = MHD_start_daemon(0, 8080, NULL, NULL, dh, NULL,
                     MHD_OPTION_ARRAY, ops,
                     MHD_OPTION_END);
```

> For options that expect a single pointer argument, the second member of the **struct MHD_OptionItem** is ignored. For options that expect two pointer arguments, the first argument must be cast to **intptr_t**.

MHD_OPTION_UNESCAPE_CALLBACK

> Specify a function that should be called for unescaping escape sequences in URIs and URI arguments. Note that this function will NOT be used by the MHD_PostProcessor. If this option is not specified, the default method will be used which decodes escape sequences of the form "%HH". This option should be followed by two arguments, the first one must be of the form

```
size_t my_unescaper(void * cls, struct MHD_Connection *c, char *s)
```

> where the return value must be **strlen(s)** and **s** should be updated. Note that the unescape function must not lengthen **s** (the result must be shorter than the input and still be 0-terminated). **cls** will be set to the second argument following MHD_OPTION_UNESCAPE_CALLBACK.

MHD_OPTION_THREAD_STACK_SIZE

> Maximum stack size for threads created by MHD. This option must be followed by a **size_t**). Not specifying this option or using a value of zero means using the system default (which is likely to differ based on your platform).

MHD_OPTION_TCP_FASTQUEUE_QUEUE_SIZE

> When the flag `MHD_USE_TCP_FASTOPEN` is used, this option sets the connection handshake queue size for the TCP FASTOPEN connections. Note that a TCP FASTOPEN connection handshake occupies more resources than a TCP handshake as the SYN packets also contain DATA which is kept in the associate state until handshake is completed. If this option is not given the queue size is set to a default value of 10. This option must be followed by a **unsigned int**.

MHD_OPTION_HTTPS_MEM_DHPARAMS

> Memory pointer for the Diffie-Hellman parameters (dh.pem) to be used by the HTTPS daemon for key exchange. This option must be followed by a `const char *` argument. The argument would be a zero-terminated string with a PEM encoded PKCS3 DH parameters structure suitable for passing to `gnutls_dh_parms_import_pkcs3`.

MHD_OPTION_LISTENING_ADDRESS_REUSE

> This option must be followed by a `unsigned int` argument. If this option is present and true (nonzero) parameter is given, allow reusing the address:port of the listening socket (using `SO_REUSEPORT` on most platforms, and `SO_REUSEADDR` on Windows). If a false (zero) parameter is given, disallow reusing the the address:port of the listening socket (this usually requires no special action, but `SO_EXCLUSIVEADDRUSE` is needed on Windows). If this option is not present, default behaviour is undefined (currently, `SO_REUSEADDR` is used on all platforms, which disallows address:port reusing with the exception of Windows).

MHD_OptionItem   [C Struct]

Entry in an MHD_OPTION_ARRAY. See the `MHD_OPTION_ARRAY` option argument for its use.

The `option` member is used to specify which option is specified in the array. The other members specify the respective argument.

Note that for options taking only a single pointer, the `ptr_value` member should be set. For options taking two pointer arguments, the first pointer must be cast to `intptr_t` and both the `value` and the `ptr_value` members should be used to pass the two pointers.

MHD_ValueKind   [Enumeration]

The `MHD_ValueKind` specifies the source of the key-value pairs in the HTTP protocol.

MHD_RESPONSE_HEADER_KIND

> Response header.

MHD_HEADER_KIND

> HTTP header.

MHD_COOKIE_KIND

> Cookies. Note that the original HTTP header containing the cookie(s) will still be available and intact.

MHD_POSTDATA_KIND

> POST data. This is available only if a content encoding supported by MHD is used (currently only URL encoding), and only if the posted content fits within the available memory pool. Note that in that case, the upload data given to the `MHD_AccessHandlerCallback()` will be empty (since it has already been processed).

MHD_GET_ARGUMENT_KIND

> GET (URI) arguments.

MHD_FOOTER_KIND
> HTTP footer (only for http 1.1 chunked encodings).

MHD_RequestTerminationCode   [Enumeration]
> The MHD_RequestTerminationCode specifies reasons why a request has been termi-
> nated (or completed).

MHD_REQUEST_TERMINATED_COMPLETED_OK
> We finished sending the response.

MHD_REQUEST_TERMINATED_WITH_ERROR
> Error handling the connection (resources exhausted, other side closed
> connection, application error accepting request, etc.)

MHD_REQUEST_TERMINATED_TIMEOUT_REACHED
> No activity on the connection for the number of seconds specified using
> MHD_OPTION_CONNECTION_TIMEOUT.

MHD_REQUEST_TERMINATED_DAEMON_SHUTDOWN
> We had to close the session since MHD was being shut down.

MHD_ResponseMemoryMode   [Enumeration]
> The MHD_ResponeMemoryMode specifies how MHD should treat the memory buffer
> given for the response in MHD_create_response_from_buffer.

MHD_RESPMEM_PERSISTENT
> Buffer is a persistent (static/global) buffer that won't change for at least
> the lifetime of the response, MHD should just use it, not free it, not copy
> it, just keep an alias to it.

MHD_RESPMEM_MUST_FREE
> Buffer is heap-allocated with malloc (or equivalent) and should be freed
> by MHD after processing the response has concluded (response reference
> counter reaches zero).

MHD_RESPMEM_MUST_COPY
> Buffer is in transient memory, but not on the heap (for example, on the
> stack or non-malloc allocated) and only valid during the call to MHD_
> create_response_from_buffer. MHD must make its own private copy
> of the data for processing.

MHD_ResponseFlags   [Enumeration]
> Response-specific flags. Passed as an argument to MHD_set_response_options().

MHD_RF_NONE
> No special handling.

MHD_RF_HTTP_VERSION_1_0_ONLY
> Only respond in conservative HTTP 1.0-mode. In particular, do not (au-
> tomatically) sent "Connection" headers and always close the connection
> after generating the response.

MHD_ResponseOptions   [Enumeration]
>   Response-specific options. Passed in the varargs portion of `MHD_set_response_options()`.

>   MHD_RO_END
>>   No more options / last option. This is used to terminate the VARARGs list.

3 Structures type definition

MHD_Daemon   [C Struct]
>   Handle for the daemon (listening on a socket for HTTP traffic).

MHD_Connection   [C Struct]
>   Handle for a connection / HTTP request. With HTTP/1.1, multiple requests can be
>   run over the same connection. However, MHD will only show one request per TCP
>   connection to the client at any given time.

MHD_Response   [C Struct]
>   Handle for a response.

MHD_PostProcessor   [C Struct]
>   Handle for POST processing.

MHD_ConnectionInfo   [C Union]
>   Information about a connection.

MHD_DaemonInfo   [C Union]
>   Information about an MHD daemon.

4 Callback functions definition

int *MHD_AcceptPolicyCallback (*void *cls, const struct*   [Function Pointer]
  *sockaddr * addr, socklen_t addrlen*)
  Invoked in the context of a connection to allow or deny a client to connect. This
  callback return MHD_YES if connection is allowed, MHD_NO if not.

  cls   custom value selected at callback registration time;

  addr   address information from the client;

  addrlen length of the address information.

int *MHD_AccessHandlerCallback (*void *cls, struct*   [Function Pointer]
  *MHD_Connection * connection, const char *url, const char *method, const char*
  *version, const char *upload_data, size_t *upload_data_size, void **con_cls*)
  Invoked in the context of a connection to answer a request from the client. This
  callback must call MHD functions (example: the MHD_Response ones) to provide
  content to give back to the client and return an HTTP status code (i.e. 200 for OK,
  404, etc.).

  Chapter 11 [microhttpd-post], page 36, for details on how to code this callback.

  Must return MHD_YES if the connection was handled successfully, MHD_NO if the socket
  must be closed due to a serious error while handling the request

  cls   custom value selected at callback registration time;

  url   the URL requested by the client;

  method the HTTP method used by the client (GET, PUT, DELETE, POST, etc.);

  version the HTTP version string (i.e. HTTP/1.1);

  upload_data
      the data being uploaded (excluding headers):

      POST data **will** be made available incrementally in *upload_data*; even if
      POST data is available, the first time the callback is invoked there won't
      be upload data, as this is done just after MHD parses the headers. If
      supported by the client and the HTTP version, the application can at
      this point queue an error response to possibly avoid the upload entirely.
      If no response is generated, MHD will (if required) automatically send a
      100 CONTINUE reply to the client.

      Afterwards, POST data will be passed to the callback to be processed
      incrementally by the application. The application may return MHD_NO
      to forcefully terminate the TCP connection without generating a proper
      HTTP response. Once all of the upload data has been provided to the
      application, the application will be called again with 0 bytes of upload
      data. At this point, a response should be queued to complete the handling
      of the request.

upload_data_size
> set initially to the size of the *upload_data* provided; this callback must update this value to the number of bytes **NOT** processed; unless external select is used, the callback maybe required to process at least some data. If the callback fails to process data in multi-threaded or internal-select mode and if the read-buffer is already at the maximum size that MHD is willing to use for reading (about half of the maximum amount of memory allowed for the connection), then MHD will abort handling the connection and return an internal server error to the client. In order to avoid this, clients must be able to process upload data incrementally and reduce the value of `upload_data_size`.

con_cls
> reference to a pointer, initially set to `NULL`, that this callback can set to some address and that will be preserved by MHD for future calls for this request;

> since the access handler may be called many times (i.e., for a `PUT`/`POST` operation with plenty of upload data) this allows the application to easily associate some request-specific state;

> if necessary, this state can be cleaned up in the global `MHD_RequestCompletedCallback` (which can be set with the `MHD_OPTION_NOTIFY_COMPLETED`).

`void *MHD_RequestCompletedCallback` (*void *cls, struct*   [Function Pointer]
    MHD_Connectionconnection, void **con_cls, enum
    MHD_RequestTerminationCode toe)

Signature of the callback used by MHD to notify the application about completed requests.

cls
> custom value selected at callback registration time;

connection
> connection handle;

con_cls
> value as set by the last call to the `MHD_AccessHandlerCallback`;

toe
> reason for request termination see `MHD_OPTION_NOTIFY_COMPLETED`.

`int *MHD_KeyValueIterator` (*void *cls, enum MHD_ValueKind*   [Function Pointer]
    kind, const char *key, const char *value)

Iterator over key-value pairs. This iterator can be used to iterate over all of the cookies, headers, or `POST`-data fields of a request, and also to iterate over the headers that have been added to a response.

cls
> custom value specified when iteration was triggered;

kind
> kind of the header we are looking at

key
> key for the value, can be an empty string

value
> value corresponding value, can be NULL

Return `MHD_YES` to continue iterating, `MHD_NO` to abort the iteration.

`int *MHD_ContentReaderCallback` (*void *cls, uint64_t pos,*   [Function Pointer]
       char *buf, size_t max)

Callback used by MHD in order to obtain content. The callback has to copy at most *max* bytes of content into *buf*. The total number of bytes that has been placed into *buf* should be returned.

Note that returning zero will cause MHD to try again. Thus, returning zero should only be used in conjunction with `MHD_suspend_connection()` to avoid busy waiting.

While usually the callback simply returns the number of bytes written into *buf*, there are two special return value:

`MHD_CONTENT_READER_END_OF_STREAM` (-1) should be returned for the regular end of transmission (with chunked encoding, MHD will then terminate the chunk and send any HTTP footers that might be present; without chunked encoding and given an unknown response size, MHD will simply close the connection; note that while returning `MHD_CONTENT_READER_END_OF_STREAM` is not technically legal if a response size was specified, MHD accepts this and treats it just as `MHD_CONTENT_READER_END_WITH_ERROR`.

`MHD_CONTENT_READER_END_WITH_ERROR` (-2) is used to indicate a server error generating the response; this will cause MHD to simply close the connection immediately. If a response size was given or if chunked encoding is in use, this will indicate an error to the client. Note, however, that if the client does not know a response size and chunked encoding is not in use, then clients will not be able to tell the difference between `MHD_CONTENT_READER_END_WITH_ERROR` and `MHD_CONTENT_READER_END_OF_STREAM`. This is not a limitation of MHD but rather of the HTTP protocol.

    cls   custom value selected at callback registration time;

    pos   position in the datastream to access; note that if an `MHD_Response` object is re-used, it is possible for the same content reader to be queried multiple times for the same data; however, if an `MHD_Response` is not re-used, MHD guarantees that *pos* will be the sum of all non-negative return values obtained from the content reader so far.

Return `-1` on error (MHD will no longer try to read content and instead close the connection with the client).

`void *MHD_ContentReaderFreeCallback` (*void *cls*)   [Function Pointer]

This method is called by MHD if we are done with a content reader. It should be used to free resources associated with the content reader.

`int *MHD_PostDataIterator` (*void *cls, enum MHD_ValueKind*   [Function Pointer]
       kind, const char *key, const char *filename, const char *content_type, const
       char *transfer_encoding, const char *data, uint64_t off, size_t size)

Iterator over key-value pairs where the value maybe made available in increments and/or may not be zero-terminated. Used for processing `POST` data.

    cls   custom value selected at callback registration time;

    kind   type of the value;

    key   zero-terminated key for the value;

filename name of the uploaded file, `NULL` if not known;

content_type
   mime-type of the data, `NULL` if not known;

transfer_encoding
   encoding of the data, `NULL` if not known;

data pointer to size bytes of data at the specified offset;

off offset of data in the overall value;

size number of bytes in data available.

Return `MHD_YES` to continue iterating, `MHD_NO` to abort the iteration.

5 Starting and stopping the server

void MHD_set_panic_func (*MHD_PanicCallback cb, void *cls*)   [Function]
    Set a handler for fatal errors.

    cb   function to call if MHD encounters a fatal internal error. If no handler
                       was set explicitly, MHD will call `abort`.

    cls   closure argument for cb; the other arguments are the name of the source
                       file, line number and a string describing the nature of the fatal error
                       (which can be `NULL`)

struct MHD_Daemon * MHD_start_daemon (*unsigned int flags,*   [Function]
        *unsigned short port, MHD_AcceptPolicyCallback apc, void *apc_cls,*
        *MHD_AccessHandlerCallback dh, void *dh_cls, ...*)
    Start a webserver on the given port.

    flags   OR-ed combination of `MHD_FLAG` values;

    port   port to bind to;

    apc   callback to call to check which clients will be allowed to connect; you can
                       pass `NULL` in which case connections from any IP will be accepted;

    apc_cls   extra argument to *apc*;

    dh   default handler for all URIs;

    dh_cls   extra argument to *dh*.

    Additional arguments are a list of options (type-value pairs, terminated with `MHD_`
    `OPTION_END`). It is mandatory to use `MHD_OPTION_END` as last argument, even when
    there are no additional arguments.

    Return `NULL` on error, handle to daemon on success.

int MHD_quiesce_daemon (*struct MHD_Daemon *daemon*)   [Function]
    Stop accepting connections from the listening socket. Allows clients to continue pro-
    cessing, but stops accepting new connections. Note that the caller is responsible for
    closing the returned socket; however, if MHD is run using threads (anything but ex-
    ternal select mode), it must not be closed until AFTER `MHD_stop_daemon` has been
    called (as it is theoretically possible that an existing thread is still using it).

    This function is useful in the special case that a listen socket is to be migrated to
    another process (i.e. a newer version of the HTTP server) while existing connections
    should continue to be processed until they are finished.

    Return `-1` on error (daemon not listening), the handle to the listen socket otherwise.

void MHD_stop_daemon (*struct MHD_Daemon *daemon*)   [Function]
    Shutdown an HTTP daemon.

int MHD_run (*struct MHD_Daemon *daemon*)   [Function]
> Run webserver operations (without blocking unless in client callbacks). This
> method should be called by clients in combination with `MHD_get_fdset()` if the
> client-controlled `select`-method is used.
>
> This function will work for external `poll` and `select` mode. However, if using external
> `select` mode, you may want to instead use `MHD_run_from_select`, as it is more
> efficient.
>
> *daemon*   daemon to process connections of
>
> Return `MHD_YES` on success, `MHD_NO` if this daemon was not started with the right
> options for this call.

int MHD_run_from_select (*struct MHD_Daemon *daemon, const fd_set*   [Function]
>   **read_fd_set*, const fd_set *write_fd_set, const fd_set *except_fd_set*)
> Run webserver operations given sets of ready socket handles.
>
> This method should be called by clients in combination with `MHD_get_fdset` if the
> client-controlled (external) select method is used.
>
> You can use this function instead of `MHD_run` if you called `select` on the result from
> `MHD_get_fdset`. File descriptors in the sets that are not controlled by MHD will be
> ignored. Calling this function instead of `MHD_run` is more efficient as MHD will not
> have to call `select` again to determine which operations are ready.
>
> *daemon*   daemon to process connections of
>
> *read_fd_set*
> >   set of descriptors that must be ready for reading without blocking
>
> *write_fd_set*
> >   set of descriptors that must be ready for writing without blocking
>
> *except_fd_set*
> >   ignored, can be NULL
>
> Return `MHD_YES` on success, `MHD_NO` on serious internal errors.

void MHD_add_connection (*struct MHD_Daemon *daemon, int*   [Function]
>   *client_socket, const struct sockaddr *addr, socklen_t addrlen*)
> Add another client connection to the set of connections managed by MHD. This
> API is usually not needed (since MHD will accept inbound connections on the server
> socket). Use this API in special cases, for example if your HTTP server is behind
> NAT and needs to connect out to the HTTP client, or if you are building a proxy.
>
> If you use this API in conjunction with a internal select or a thread pool, you must set
> the option `MHD_USE_PIPE_FOR_SHUTDOWN` to ensure that the freshly added connection
> is immediately processed by MHD.
>
> The given client socket will be managed (and closed!) by MHD after this call and
> must no longer be used directly by the application afterwards.
>
> *daemon*   daemon that manages the connection

client_socket
               socket to manage (MHD will expect to receive an HTTP request from this socket next).

addr   IP address of the client

addrlen   number of bytes in addr

This function will return `MHD_YES` on success, `MHD_NO` if this daemon could not handle the connection (i.e. malloc failed, etc). The socket will be closed in any case; 'errno' is set to indicate further details about the error.

6 Implementing external `select`

`int` `MHD_get_fdset` (*struct MHD_Daemon *daemon, fd_set **   [Function]
     read_fd_set, fd_set * write_fd_set, fd_set * except_fd_set, int *max_fd)
> Obtain the `select()` sets for this daemon. The daemon's socket is added to
> *read_fd_set*. The list of currently existent connections is scanned and their file
> descriptors added to the correct set.
>
> After the call completed successfully: the variable referenced by *max_fd* references
> the file descriptor with highest integer identifier. The variable must be set to zero
> before invoking this function.
>
> Return `MHD_YES` on success, `MHD_NO` if: the arguments are invalid (example: `NULL`
> pointers); this daemon was not started with the right options for this call.

`int` `MHD_get_timeout` (*struct MHD_Daemon *daemon, unsigned long*   [Function]
     long *timeout)
> Obtain timeout value for select for this daemon (only needed if connection timeout
> is used). The returned value is how many milliseconds `select` should at most block,
> not the timeout value set for connections. This function must not be called if the
> `MHD_USE_THREAD_PER_CONNECTION` mode is in use (since then it is not meaningful to
> ask for a timeout, after all, there is concurrenct activity). The function must also not
> be called by user-code if `MHD_USE_INTERNAL_SELECT` is in use. In the latter case, the
> behavior is undefined.
>
> *daemon*   which daemon to obtain the timeout from.
>
> *timeout*   will be set to the timeout (in milliseconds).
>
> Return `MHD_YES` on success, `MHD_NO` if timeouts are not used (or no connections exist
> that would necessiate the use of a timeout right now).

7 Handling requests

int MHD_get_connection_values (*struct MHD_Connection*   [Function]
       *connection, enum MHD_ValueKind kind, MHD_KeyValueIterator iterator,
       void *iterator_cls*)
Get all the headers matching *kind* from the request.

The *iterator* callback is invoked once for each header, with *iterator_cls* as first argument. After version 0.9.19, the headers are iterated in the same order as they were received from the network; previous versions iterated over the headers in reverse order.

MHD_get_connection_values returns the number of entries iterated over; this can be less than the number of headers if, while iterating, *iterator* returns MHD_NO.

iterator can be NULL: in this case this function just counts and returns the number of headers.

In the case of MHD_GET_ARGUMENT_KIND, the *value* argument will be NULL if the URL contained a key without an equals operator. For example, for a HTTP request to the URL "http://foo/bar?key", the *value* argument is NULL; in contrast, a HTTP request to the URL "http://foo/bar?key=", the *value* argument is the empty string. The normal case is that the URL contains "http://foo/bar?key=value" in which case *value* would be the string "value" and *key* would contain the string "key".

int MHD_set_connection_value (*struct MHD_Connection *connection,*   [Function]
       *enum MHD_ValueKind kind, const char * key, const char * value*)
This function can be used to append an entry to the list of HTTP headers of a connection (so that the MHD_get_connection_values function will return them – and the MHD PostProcessor will also see them). This maybe required in certain situations (see Mantis #1399) where (broken) HTTP implementations fail to supply values needed by the post processor (or other parts of the application).

This function MUST only be called from within the MHD_AccessHandlerCallback (otherwise, access maybe improperly synchronized). Furthermore, the client must guarantee that the key and value arguments are 0-terminated strings that are NOT freed until the connection is closed. (The easiest way to do this is by passing only arguments to permanently allocated strings.).

connection is the connection for which the entry for *key* of the given *kind* should be set to the given *value*.

The function returns MHD_NO if the operation could not be performed due to insufficient memory and MHD_YES on success.

const char * MHD_lookup_connection_value (*struct*   [Function]
       *MHD_Connection *connection, enum MHD_ValueKind kind, const char *key*)
Get a particular header value. If multiple values match the *kind*, return one of them (the "first", whatever that means). *key* must reference a zero-terminated ASCII-coded string representing the header to look for: it is compared against the headers using strcasecmp(), so case is ignored. A value of NULL for *key* can be used to lookup 'trailing' values without a key, for example if a URI is of the form

"http://example.com/?trailer", a *key* of `NULL` can be used to access "tailer" The function returns `NULL` if no matching item was found.

8 Building responses to requests

Response objects handling by MHD is asynchronous with respect to the application execution flow. Instances of the `MHD_Response` structure are not associated to a daemon and neither to a client connection: they are managed with reference counting.

In the simplest case: we allocate a new `MHD_Response` structure for each response, we use it once and finally we destroy it.

MHD allows more efficient resources usages.

Example: we allocate a new `MHD_Response` structure for each response **kind**, we use it every time we have to give that response and we finally destroy it only when the daemon shuts down.

8.1 Enqueuing a response

`int MHD_queue_response` (*struct MHD_Connection *connection,*   [Function]
        unsigned int status_code, struct MHD_Response *response)
> Queue a response to be transmitted to the client as soon as possible but only after MHD_AccessHandlerCallback returns. This function checks that it is legal to queue a response at this time for the given connection. It also increments the internal reference counter for the response object (the counter will be decremented automatically once the response has been transmitted).

> *connection*
>> the connection identifying the client;

> *status_code*
>> HTTP status code (i.e. 200 for OK);

> *response*   response to transmit.

> Return `MHD_YES` on success or if message has been queued. Return `MHD_NO`: if arguments are invalid (example: `NULL` pointer); on error (i.e. reply already sent).

`void MHD_destroy_response` (*struct MHD_Response *response*)   [Function]
> Destroy a response object and associated resources (decrement the reference counter). Note that MHD may keep some of the resources around if the response is still in the queue for some clients, so the memory may not necessarily be freed immediately.

An explanation of reference counting[1]:

1. a `MHD_Response` object is allocated:
   ```
   struct MHD_Response * response = MHD_create_response_from_buffer(...);
   /* here: reference counter = 1 */
   ```
2. the `MHD_Response` object is enqueued in a `MHD_Connection`:
   ```
   MHD_queue_response(connection, , response);
   /* here: reference counter = 2 */
   ```

---

[1] Note to readers acquainted to the Tcl API: reference counting on `MHD_Connection` structures is handled in the same way as Tcl handles `Tcl_Obj` structures through `Tcl_IncrRefCount()` and `Tcl_DecrRefCount()`.

3. the creator of the response object discharges responsibility for it:

```
MHD_destroy_response(response);
/* here: reference counter = 1 */
```

4. the daemon handles the connection sending the response's data to the client then decrements the reference counter by calling `MHD_destroy_response()`: the counter's value drops to zero and the `MHD_Response` object is released.

8.2 Creating a response object

struct MHD_Response * MHD_create_response_from_callback   [Function]
          (*uint64_t size, size_t block_size, MHD_ContentReaderCallback crc, void
          crc_cls, MHD_ContentReaderFreeCallback crfc)
     Create a response object. The response object can be extended with header information and then it can be used any number of times.

     size   size of the data portion of the response, `-1` for unknown;

     block_size   preferred block size for querying *crc* (advisory only, MHD may still call *crc* using smaller chunks); this is essentially the buffer size used for IO, clients should pick a value that is appropriate for IO and memory performance requirements;

     crc   callback to use to obtain response data;

     crc_cls   extra argument to *crc*;

     crfc   callback to call to free *crc_cls* resources.

     Return `NULL` on error (i.e. invalid arguments, out of memory).

struct MHD_Response * MHD_create_response_from_fd (*uint64_t*   [Function]
          size, int fd)
     Create a response object. The response object can be extended with header information and then it can be used any number of times.

     size   size of the data portion of the response (should be smaller or equal to the size of the file)

     fd   file descriptor referring to a file on disk with the data; will be closed when response is destroyed; note that 'fd' must be an actual file descriptor (not a pipe or socket) since MHD might use 'sendfile' or 'seek' on it. The descriptor should be in blocking-IO mode.

     Return `NULL` on error (i.e. invalid arguments, out of memory).

struct MHD_Response *   [Function]
          MHD_create_response_from_fd_at_offset (*size_t size, int fd, off_t offset*)
     Create a response object. The response object can be extended with header information and then it can be used any number of times. Note that you need to be a bit careful about `off_t` when writing this code. Depending on your platform, MHD is likely to have been compiled with support for 64-bit files. When you compile your

own application, you must make sure that `off_t` is also a 64-bit value. If not, your compiler may pass a 32-bit value as `off_t`, which will result in 32-bits of garbage.

If you use the autotools, use the `AC_SYS_LARGEFILE` autoconf macro and make sure to include the generated `config.h` file before `microhttpd.h` to avoid problems. If you do not have a build system and only want to run on a GNU/Linux system, you could also use

```
#define _FILE_OFFSET_BITS 64
#include <sys/types.h>
#include <sys/stat.h>
#include <fcntl.h>
#include <microhttpd.h>
```

to ensure 64-bit `off_t`. Note that if your operating system does not support 64-bit files, MHD will be compiled with a 32-bit `off_t` (in which case the above would be wrong).

size   size of the data portion of the response (number of bytes to transmit from the file starting at offset).

fd   file descriptor referring to a file on disk with the data; will be closed when response is destroyed; note that 'fd' must be an actual file descriptor (not a pipe or socket) since MHD might use 'sendfile' or 'seek' on it. The descriptor should be in blocking-IO mode.

offset   offset to start reading from in the file

Return `NULL` on error (i.e. invalid arguments, out of memory).

struct MHD_Response * MHD_create_response_from_buffer   [Function]
        (*size_t size, void *data, enum MHD_ResponseMemoryMode mode*)
Create a response object. The response object can be extended with header information and then it can be used any number of times.

size   size of the data portion of the response;

buffer   the data itself;

mode   memory management options for buffer; use MHD_RESPMEM_PERSISTENT if the buffer is static/global memory, use MHD_RESPMEM_MUST_FREE if the buffer is heap-allocated and should be freed by MHD and MHD_RESPMEM_MUST_COPY if the buffer is in transient memory (i.e. on the stack) and must be copied by MHD;

Return `NULL` on error (i.e. invalid arguments, out of memory).

struct MHD_Response * MHD_create_response_from_data (*size_t*   [Function]
        size, void *data, int must_free, int must_copy)
Create a response object. The response object can be extended with header information and then it can be used any number of times. This function is deprecated, use `MHD_create_response_from_buffer` instead.

size   size of the data portion of the response;

data   the data itself;

must_free   if true: MHD should free data when done;

must_copy

> if true: MHD allocates a block of memory and use it to make a copy
> of *data* embedded in the returned `MHD_Response` structure; handling of
> the embedded memory is responsibility of MHD; *data* can be released
> anytime after this call returns.

Return `NULL` on error (i.e. invalid arguments, out of memory).

Example: create a response from a statically allocated string:

```
const char * data = "<html><body><p>Error!</p></body></html>";

struct MHD_Connection * connection = ...;
struct MHD_Response *   response;

response = MHD_create_response_from_buffer (strlen(data), data,
                                    MHD_RESPMEM_PERSISTENT);
MHD_queue_response(connection, 404, response);
MHD_destroy_response(response);
```

8.3 Adding headers to a response

int `MHD_add_response_header` (*struct MHD_Response *response,*   [Function]
        *const char *header, const char *content*)

Add a header line to the response. The strings referenced by *header* and *content*
must be zero-terminated and they are duplicated into memory blocks embedded in
response.

Notice that the strings must not hold newlines, carriage returns or tab chars.

Return `MHD_NO` on error (i.e. invalid header or content format or memory allocation
error).

int `MHD_add_response_footer` (*struct MHD_Response *response,*   [Function]
        *const char *footer, const char *content*)

Add a footer line to the response. The strings referenced by *footer* and *content*
must be zero-terminated and they are duplicated into memory blocks embedded in
response.

Notice that the strings must not hold newlines, carriage returns or tab chars. You
can add response footers at any time before signalling the end of the response to
MHD (not just before calling 'MHD_queue_response'). Footers are useful for adding
cryptographic checksums to the reply or to signal errors encountered during data
generation. This call was introduced in MHD 0.9.3.

Return `MHD_NO` on error (i.e. invalid header or content format or memory allocation
error).

int `MHD_del_response_header` (*struct MHD_Response *response,*   [Function]
        *const char *header, const char *content*)

Delete a header (or footer) line from the response. Return `MHD_NO` on error (arguments
are invalid or no such header known).

8.4 Setting response options

int MHD_set_response_options (*struct MHD_Response *response,*   [Function]
      enum MHD_ResponseFlags flags, ...)

Set special flags and options for a response.

Calling this functions sets the given flags and options for the response.

response   which response should be modified;

flags   flags to set for the response;

Additional arguments are a list of options (type-value pairs, terminated with MHD_RO_END). It is mandatory to use MHD_RO_END as last argument, even when there are no additional arguments.

Return MHD_NO on error, MHD_YES on success.

8.5 Inspecting a response object

int MHD_get_response_headers (*struct MHD_Response *response,*   [Function]
      *MHD_KeyValueIterator iterator, void *iterator_cls*)

Get all of the headers added to a response.

Invoke the *iterator* callback for each header in the response, using *iterator_cls* as first argument. Return number of entries iterated over. *iterator* can be NULL: in this case the function just counts headers.

iterator should not modify the its key and value arguments, unless we know what we are doing.

const char * MHD_get_response_header (*struct MHD_Response*   [Function]
      *response, const char *key)

Find and return a pointer to the value of a particular header from the response. *key* must reference a zero-terminated string representing the header to look for. The search is case sensitive. Return NULL if header does not exist or *key* is NULL.

We should not modify the value, unless we know what we are doing.

9 Flow control.

Sometimes it may be possible that clients upload data faster than an application can process it, or that an application needs an extended period of time to generate a response. If MHD_ USE_THREAD_PER_CONNECTION is used, applications can simply deal with this by performing their logic within the thread and thus effectively blocking connection processing by MHD. In all other modes, blocking logic must not be placed within the callbacks invoked by MHD as this would also block processing of other requests, as a single thread may be responsible for tens of thousands of connections.

Instead, applications using thread modes other than MHD_USE_THREAD_PER_CONNECTION should use the following functions to perform flow control.

int MHD_suspend_connection (*struct MHD_Connection *connection*)   [Function]
> Suspend handling of network data for a given connection. This can be used to dequeue a connection from MHD's event loop (external select, internal select or thread pool; not applicable to thread-per-connection!) for a while.
>
> If you use this API in conjunction with a internal select or a thread pool, you must set the option MHD_USE_SUSPEND_RESUME to ensure that a resumed connection is immediately processed by MHD.
>
> Suspended connections continue to count against the total number of connections allowed (per daemon, as well as per IP, if such limits are set). Suspended connections will NOT time out; timeouts will restart when the connection handling is resumed. While a connection is suspended, MHD will not detect disconnects by the client.
>
> The only safe time to suspend a connection is from the MHD_AccessHandlerCallback.
>
> Finally, it is an API violation to call MHD_stop_daemon while having suspended connections (this will at least create memory and socket leaks or lead to undefined behavior). You must explicitly resume all connections before stopping the daemon.
>
> *connection*
>> the connection to suspend

int MHD_resume_connection (*struct MHD_Connection *connection*)   [Function]
> Resume handling of network data for suspended connection. It is safe to resume a suspended connection at any time. Calling this function on a connection that was not previously suspended will result in undefined behavior.
>
> *connection*
>> the connection to resume

10 Utilizing Authentication

MHD support three types of client authentication.

Basic authentication uses a simple authentication method based on BASE64 algorithm. Username and password are exchanged in clear between the client and the server, so this method must only be used for non-sensitive content or when the session is protected with https. When using basic authentication MHD will have access to the clear password, possibly allowing to create a chained authentication toward an external authentication server.

Digest authentication uses a one-way authentication method based on MD5 hash algorithm. Only the hash will transit over the network, hence protecting the user password. The nonce will prevent replay attacks. This method is appropriate for general use, especially when https is not used to encrypt the session.

Client certificate authentication uses a X.509 certificate from the client. This is the strongest authentication mechanism but it requires the use of HTTPS. Client certificate authentication can be used simultaneously with Basic or Digest Authentication in order to provide a two levels authentication (like for instance separate machine and user authentication). A code example for using client certificates is presented in the MHD tutorial.

10.1 Using Basic Authentication

char * MHD_basic_auth_get_username_password (*struct*   [Function]
     MHD_Connection *connection, char** password)
> Get the username and password from the basic authorization header sent by the client. Return `NULL` if no username could be found, a pointer to the username if found. If returned value is not `NULL`, the value must be `free()`'ed.
>
> *password* reference a buffer to store the password. It can be `NULL`. If returned value is not `NULL`, the value must be `free()`'ed.

int MHD_queue_basic_auth_fail_response (*struct MHD_Connection*   [Function]
     *connection, const char *realm, struct MHD_Response *response)
> Queues a response to request basic authentication from the client. Return `MHD_YES` if successful, otherwise `MHD_NO`.
>
> *realm* must reference to a zero-terminated string representing the realm.
>
> *response* a response structure to specify what shall be presented to the client with a 401 HTTP status.

10.2 Using Digest Authentication

char * MHD_digest_auth_get_username (*struct MHD_Connection*   [Function]
     *connection)
> Find and return a pointer to the username value from the request header. Return `NULL` if the value is not found or header does not exist. If returned value is not `NULL`, the value must be `free()`'ed.

int MHD_digest_auth_check (*struct MHD_Connection *connection,*   [Function]
        *const char *realm, const char *username, const char *password, unsigned int*
        nonce_timeout)

> Checks if the provided values in the WWW-Authenticate header are valid and sound according to RFC2716. If valid return MHD_YES, otherwise return MHD_NO.
>
> *realm* must reference to a zero-terminated string representing the realm.
>
> *username* must reference to a zero-terminated string representing the username, it is usually the returned value from MHD_digest_auth_get_username.
>
> *password* must reference to a zero-terminated string representing the password, most probably it will be the result of a lookup of the username against a local database.
>
> *nonce_timeout* is the amount of time in seconds for a nonce to be invalid. Most of the time it is sound to specify 300 seconds as its values.

int MHD_queue_auth_fail_response (*struct MHD_Connection*   [Function]
        *connection, const char *realm, const char *opaque, struct MHD_Response*
        response, int signal_stale)

> Queues a response to request authentication from the client, return MHD_YES if successful, otherwise MHD_NO.
>
> *realm* must reference to a zero-terminated string representing the realm.
>
> *opaque* must reference to a zero-terminated string representing a value that gets passed to the client and expected to be passed again to the server as-is. This value can be a hexadecimal or base64 string.
>
> *response* a response structure to specify what shall be presented to the client with a 401 HTTP status.
>
> *signal_stale* a value that signals "stale=true" in the response header to indicate the invalidity of the nonce and no need to ask for authentication parameters and only a new nonce gets generated. MHD_YES to generate a new nonce, MHD_NO to ask for authentication parameters.

Example: handling digest authentication requests and responses.

```
#define PAGE "<html><head><title>libmicrohttpd demo</title></head><body>Access granted</body></html>"
#define DENIED "<html><head><title>libmicrohttpd demo</title></head><body>Access denied</body></html>"
#define OPAQUE "11733b200778ce33060f31c9af70a870ba96ddd4"

static int
ahc_echo (void *cls,
          struct MHD_Connection *connection,
          const char *url,
          const char *method,
          const char *version,
          const char *upload_data, size_t *upload_data_size, void **ptr)
{
  struct MHD_Response *response;
  char *username;
  const char *password = "testpass";
```

```
      const char *realm = "test@example.com";
      int ret;

      username = MHD_digest_auth_get_username(connection);
      if (username == NULL)
        {
          response = MHD_create_response_from_buffer(strlen (DENIED),
              DENIED,
              MHD_RESPMEM_PERSISTENT);
          ret = MHD_queue_auth_fail_response(connection, realm,
OPAQUE,
response,
MHD_NO);
          MHD_destroy_response(response);
          return ret;
        }
      ret = MHD_digest_auth_check(connection, realm,
          username,
          password,
          300);
      free(username);
      if ( (ret == MHD_INVALID_NONCE) ||
           (ret == MHD_NO) )
        {
          response = MHD_create_response_from_buffer(strlen (DENIED),
              DENIED,
              MHD_RESPMEM_PERSISTENT);
          if (NULL == response)
return MHD_NO;
          ret = MHD_queue_auth_fail_response(connection, realm,
OPAQUE,
response,
(ret == MHD_INVALID_NONCE) ? MHD_YES : MHD_NO);
          MHD_destroy_response(response);
          return ret;
        }
      response = MHD_create_response_from_buffer (strlen(PAGE), PAGE,
          MHD_RESPMEM_PERSISTENT);
      ret = MHD_queue_response(connection, MHD_HTTP_OK, response);
      MHD_destroy_response(response);
      return ret;
}
```

11 Adding a POST processor

MHD provides the post processor API to make it easier for applications to parse the data of a client's POST request: the `MHD_AccessHandlerCallback` will be invoked multiple times to process data as it arrives; at each invocation a new chunk of data must be processed. The arguments *upload_data* and *upload_data_size* are used to reference the chunk of data.

When `MHD_AccessHandlerCallback` is invoked for a new connection: its **con_cls* argument is set to NULL. When POST data comes in the upload buffer it is **mandatory** to use the *con_cls* to store a reference to per-connection data. The fact that the pointer was initially NULL can be used to detect that this is a new request.

One method to detect that a new connection was established is to set **con_cls* to an unused integer:

```
int
access_handler (void *cls,
                struct MHD_Connection * connection,
                const char *url,
                const char *method, const char *version,
                const char *upload_data, size_t *upload_data_size,
                void **con_cls)
{
  static int old_connection_marker;
  int new_connection = (NULL == *con_cls);

  if (new_connection)
    {
      /* new connection with POST */
      *con_cls = &old_connection_marker;
    }


  ...
}
```

In contrast to the previous example, for POST requests in particular, it is more common to use the value of `*con_cls` to keep track of actual state used during processing, such as the post processor (or a struct containing a post processor):

```
int
access_handler (void *cls,
                struct MHD_Connection * connection,
                const char *url,
                const char *method, const char *version,
                const char *upload_data, size_t *upload_data_size,
                void **con_cls)
{
  struct MHD_PostProcessor * pp = *con_cls;

  if (pp == NULL)
    {
```

```
        pp = MHD_create_post_processor(connection, ...);
        *con_cls = pp;
        return MHD_YES;
      }
    if (*upload_data_size)
      {
        MHD_post_process(pp, upload_data, *upload_data_size);
        *upload_data_size = 0;
        return MHD_YES;
      }
    else
      {
        MHD_destroy_post_processor(pp);
        return MHD_queue_response(...);
      }
  }
```

Note that the callback from `MHD_OPTION_NOTIFY_COMPLETED` should be used to destroy the post processor. This cannot be done inside of the access handler since the connection may not always terminate normally.

11.1 Programming interface for the POST processor

`struct MHD_PostProcessor * MHD_create_post_processor` (*struct*   [Function]
      *MHD_Connection *connection, size_t buffer_size, MHD_PostDataIterator*
      *iterator, void *iterator_cls*)

Create a PostProcessor. A PostProcessor can be used to (incrementally) parse the data portion of a POST request.

connection
        the connection on which the POST is happening (used to determine the POST format);

buffer_size maximum number of bytes to use for internal buffering (used only for the parsing, specifically the parsing of the keys). A tiny value (256-1024) should be sufficient; do **NOT** use a value smaller than 256; for good performance, use 32k or 64k (i.e. 65536).

iterator iterator to be called with the parsed data; must **NOT** be NULL;

iterator_cls
        custom value to be used as first argument to *iterator*.

Return NULL on error (out of memory, unsupported encoding), otherwise a PP handle.

`int MHD_post_process` (*struct MHD_PostProcessor *pp, const char*   [Function]
      *post_data, size_t post_data_len)

Parse and process POST data. Call this function when POST data is available (usually during an `MHD_AccessHandlerCallback`) with the *upload_data* and *upload_data_size*. Whenever possible, this will then cause calls to the `MHD_IncrementalKeyValueIterator`.

pp   the post processor;

post_data   *post_data_len* bytes of POST data;

post_data_len
              length of *post_data*.

Return MHD_YES on success, MHD_NO on error (out-of-memory, iterator aborted, parse error).

int **MHD_destroy_post_processor** (*struct MHD_PostProcessor *pp*)   [Function]
Release PostProcessor resources. After this function is being called, the PostProcessor is guaranteed to no longer call its iterator. There is no special call to the iterator to indicate the end of the post processing stream. After destroying the PostProcessor, the programmer should perform any necessary work to complete the processing of the iterator.

Return MHD_YES if processing completed nicely, MHD_NO if there were spurious characters or formatting problems with the post request. It is common to ignore the return value of this function.

12 Obtaining and modifying status information.

12.1 Obtaining state information about an MHD daemon

`const union MHD_DaemonInfo * MHD_get_daemon_info` (*struct*   [Function]
     *MHD_Daemon *daemon, enum MHD_DaemonInfoType infoType, ...*)
  Obtain information about the given daemon. This function is currently not fully implemented.

  daemon   the daemon about which information is desired;

  infoType   type of information that is desired

  ...   additional arguments about the desired information (depending on info-Type)

  Returns a union with the respective member (depending on infoType) set to the desired information), or `NULL` in case the desired information is not available or applicable.

`MHD_DaemonInfoType`   [Enumeration]
  Values of this enum are used to specify what information about a daemon is desired.

  `MHD_DAEMON_INFO_KEY_SIZE`
          Request information about the key size for a particular cipher algorithm. The cipher algorithm should be passed as an extra argument (of type 'enum MHD_GNUTLS_CipherAlgorithm'). No longer supported, using this value will cause `MHD_get_daemon_info` to return NULL.

  `MHD_DAEMON_INFO_MAC_KEY_SIZE`
          Request information about the key size for a particular cipher algorithm. The cipher algorithm should be passed as an extra argument (of type 'enum MHD_GNUTLS_HashAlgorithm'). No longer supported, using this value will cause `MHD_get_daemon_info` to return NULL.

  `MHD_DAEMON_INFO_LISTEN_FD`
          Request the file-descriptor number that MHD is using to listen to the server socket. This can be useful if no port was specified and a client needs to learn what port is actually being used by MHD. No extra arguments should be passed.

  `MHD_DAEMON_INFO_EPOLL_FD_LINUX_ONLY`
          Request the file-descriptor number that MHD is using for epoll. If the build is not supporting epoll, NULL is returned; if we are using a thread pool or this daemon was not started with `MHD_USE_EPOLL_LINUX_ONLY`, (a pointer to) -1 is returned. If we are using `MHD_USE_SELECT_INTERNALLY` or are in 'external' select mode, the internal epoll FD is returned. This function must be used in external select mode with epoll to obtain the FD to call epoll on. No extra arguments should be passed.

MHD_DAEMON_INFO_CURRENT_CONNECTIONS

> Request the number of current connections handled by the daemon. No extra arguments should be passed and a pointer to a **union MHD_DaemonInfo** value is returned, with the **num_connections** member of type **unsigned int** set to the number of active connections.
>
> Note that in multi-threaded or internal-select mode, the real number of current connections may already be different when **MHD_get_daemon_ info** returns. The number of current connections can be used (even in multi-threaded and internal-select mode) after **MHD_quiesce_daemon** to detect whether all connections have been handled.

12.2 Obtaining state information about a connection

const union MHD_ConnectionInfo * MHD_get_connection_info   [Function]
  (*struct MHD_Connection *daemon, enum MHD_ConnectionInfoType infoType, ...*)

Obtain information about the given connection.

connection
> the connection about which information is desired;

infoType   type of information that is desired

...   additional arguments about the desired information (depending on info-Type)

Returns a union with the respective member (depending on infoType) set to the desired information), or **NULL** in case the desired information is not available or applicable.

MHD_ConnectionInfoType   [Enumeration]
  Values of this enum are used to specify what information about a connection is desired.

MHD_CONNECTION_INFO_CIPHER_ALGO
> What cipher algorithm is being used (HTTPS connections only). Takes no extra arguments. **NULL** is returned for non-HTTPS connections.

MHD_CONNECTION_INFO_PROTOCOL,
> Takes no extra arguments. Allows finding out the TLS/SSL protocol used (HTTPS connections only). **NULL** is returned for non-HTTPS connections.

MHD_CONNECTION_INFO_CLIENT_ADDRESS
> Returns information about the address of the client.   Returns essentially a **struct sockaddr **** (since the API returns a **union MHD_ConnectionInfo *** and that union contains a **struct sockaddr ***).

MHD_CONNECTION_INFO_GNUTLS_SESSION,
> Takes no extra arguments. Allows access to the underlying GNUtls session, including access to the underlying GNUtls client certificate (HTTPS connections only). Takes no extra arguments. **NULL** is returned for non-HTTPS connections.

`MHD_CONNECTION_INFO_GNUTLS_CLIENT_CERT,`
> Dysfunctional (never implemented, deprecated). Use MHD_CONNECTION_INFO_GNUTLS_SESSION to get the `gnutls_session_t` and then call `gnutls_certificate_get_peers()`.

`MHD_CONNECTION_INFO_DAEMON`
> Returns information about **struct MHD_Daemon** which manages this connection.

`MHD_CONNECTION_INFO_CONNECTION_FD`
> Returns the file descriptor (usually a TCP socket) associated with this connection (in the "connect-fd" member of the returned struct). Note that manipulating the descriptor directly can have problematic consequences (as in, break HTTP). Applications might use this access to manipulate TCP options, for example to set the "TCP-NODELAY" option for COMET-like applications. Note that MHD will set TCP-CORK after sending the HTTP header and clear it after finishing the footers automatically (if the platform supports it). As the connection callbacks are invoked in between, those might be used to set different values for TCP-CORK and TCP-NODELAY in the meantime.

12.3 Setting custom options for an individual connection

`int MHD_set_connection_option` (*struct MHD_Connection *daemon,*   [Function]
     enum MHD_CONNECTION_OPTION option, ...)
> Set a custom option for the given connection.

> *connection*
>> the connection for which an option should be set or modified;

> *option*   option to set

> ...   additional arguments for the option (depending on option)

> Returns `MHD_YES` on success, `MHD_NO` for errors (i.e. option argument invalid or option unknown).

`MHD_CONNECTION_OPTION`   [Enumeration]
> Values of this enum are used to specify which option for a connection should be changed.

> `MHD_CONNECTION_OPTION_TIMEOUT`
>> Set a custom timeout for the given connection. Specified as the number of seconds, given as an **unsigned int**. Use zero for no timeout.

13 Utility functions.

13.1 Testing for supported MHD features

`MHD_FEATURE` [Enumeration]

Values of this enum are used to specify what information about a daemon is desired.

`MHD_FEATURE_MESSAGES`

Get whether messages are supported. If supported then in debug mode messages can be printed to stderr or to external logger.

`MHD_FEATURE_SSL`

Get whether HTTPS is supported. If supported then flag MHD_USE_SSL and options MHD_OPTION_HTTPS_MEM_KEY, MHD_OPTION_HTTPS_MEM_CERT, MHD_OPTION_HTTPS_MEM_TRUST, MHD_OPTION_HTTPS_MEM_DHPARAMS, MHD_OPTION_HTTPS_CRED_TYPE, MHD_OPTION_HTTPS_PRIORITIES can be used.

`MHD_FEATURE_HTTPS_CERT_CALLBACK`

Get whether option #MHD_OPTION_HTTPS_CERT_CALLBACK is supported.

`MHD_FEATURE_IPv6`

Get whether IPv6 is supported. If supported then flag MHD_USE_IPv6 can be used.

`MHD_FEATURE_IPv6_ONLY`

Get whether IPv6 without IPv4 is supported. If not supported then IPv4 is always enabled in IPv6 sockets and flag MHD_USE_DUAL_STACK if always used when MHD_USE_IPv6 is specified.

`MHD_FEATURE_POLL`

Get whether **poll()** is supported. If supported then flag MHD_USE_POLL can be used.

`MHD_FEATURE_EPOLL`

Get whether **epoll()** is supported. If supported then Flags MHD_USE_EPOLL_LINUX_ONLY and MHD_USE_EPOLL_INTERNALLY_LINUX_ONLY can be used.

`MHD_FEATURE_SHUTDOWN_LISTEN_SOCKET`

Get whether shutdown on listen socket to signal other threads is supported. If not supported flag MHD_USE_PIPE_FOR_SHUTDOWN is automatically forced.

`MHD_FEATURE_SOCKETPAIR`

Get whether a **socketpair()** is used internally instead of a **pipe()** to signal other threads.

`MHD_FEATURE_TCP_FASTOPEN`

Get whether TCP Fast Open is supported. If supported then flag MHD_USE_TCP_FASTOPEN and option MHD_OPTION_TCP_FASTOPEN_QUEUE_SIZE can be used.

MHD_FEATURE_BASIC_AUTH

> Get whether HTTP Basic authorization is supported. If supported then functions `MHD_basic_auth_get_username_password()` and `MHD_queue_basic_auth_fail_response()` can be used.

MHD_FEATURE_DIGEST_AUTH

> Get whether HTTP Digest authorization is supported. If supported then options MHD_OPTION_DIGEST_AUTH_RANDOM, MHD_OPTION_NONCE_NC_SIZE and functions `MHD_digest_auth_check()`, can be used.

MHD_FEATURE_POSTPROCESSOR

> Get whether postprocessor is supported. If supported then functions `MHD_create_post_processor()`, `MHD_post_process()`, `MHD_destroy_post_processor()` can be used.

int MHD_is_feature_supported (*enum MHD_FEATURE feature*)   [Function]
Get information about supported MHD features. Indicate that MHD was compiled with or without support for particular feature. Some features require additional support by the kernel. However, kernel support is not checked by this function.

> *feature*   type of requested information

Returns `MHD_YES` if the feature is supported, and `MHD_NO` if not.

13.2 Unescape strings

size_t MHD_http_unescape (*char *val*)   [Function]
Process escape sequences ('%HH') Updates val in place; the result should be UTF-8 encoded and cannot be larger than the input. The result must also still be 0-terminated.

> *val*   value to unescape (modified in the process), must be a 0-terminated UTF-8 string.

Returns length of the resulting val (`strlen(val)` may be shorter afterwards due to elimination of escape sequences).

GNU-LGPL

Version 2.1, February 1999

Copyright © 1991, 1999 Free Software Foundation, Inc.
51 Franklin Street, Fifth Floor, Boston, MA 02110-1301, USA

Everyone is permitted to copy and distribute verbatim copies
of this license document, but changing it is not allowed.

[This is the first released version of the Lesser GPL. It also counts
as the successor of the GNU Library Public License, version 2, hence the
version number 2.1.]

Preamble

The licenses for most software are designed to take away your freedom to share and change
it. By contrast, the GNU General Public Licenses are intended to guarantee your freedom
to share and change free software—to make sure the software is free for all its users.

This license, the Lesser General Public License, applies to some specially designated
software—typically libraries—of the Free Software Foundation and other authors who decide
to use it. You can use it too, but we suggest you first think carefully about whether this
license or the ordinary General Public License is the better strategy to use in any particular
case, based on the explanations below.

When we speak of free software, we are referring to freedom of use, not price. Our
General Public Licenses are designed to make sure that you have the freedom to distribute
copies of free software (and charge for this service if you wish); that you receive source code
or can get it if you want it; that you can change the software and use pieces of it in new
free programs; and that you are informed that you can do these things.

To protect your rights, we need to make restrictions that forbid distributors to deny you
these rights or to ask you to surrender these rights. These restrictions translate to certain
responsibilities for you if you distribute copies of the library or if you modify it.

For example, if you distribute copies of the library, whether gratis or for a fee, you must
give the recipients all the rights that we gave you. You must make sure that they, too,
receive or can get the source code. If you link other code with the library, you must provide
complete object files to the recipients, so that they can relink them with the library after
making changes to the library and recompiling it. And you must show them these terms so
they know their rights.

We protect your rights with a two-step method: (1) we copyright the library, and (2) we
offer you this license, which gives you legal permission to copy, distribute and/or modify
the library.

To protect each distributor, we want to make it very clear that there is no warranty for
the free library. Also, if the library is modified by someone else and passed on, the recipients
should know that what they have is not the original version, so that the original author's
reputation will not be affected by problems that might be introduced by others.

Finally, software patents pose a constant threat to the existence of any free program.
We wish to make sure that a company cannot effectively restrict the users of a free program

by obtaining a restrictive license from a patent holder. Therefore, we insist that any patent license obtained for a version of the library must be consistent with the full freedom of use specified in this license.

Most GNU software, including some libraries, is covered by the ordinary GNU General Public License. This license, the GNU Lesser General Public License, applies to certain designated libraries, and is quite different from the ordinary General Public License. We use this license for certain libraries in order to permit linking those libraries into non-free programs.

When a program is linked with a library, whether statically or using a shared library, the combination of the two is legally speaking a combined work, a derivative of the original library. The ordinary General Public License therefore permits such linking only if the entire combination fits its criteria of freedom. The Lesser General Public License permits more lax criteria for linking other code with the library.

We call this license the *Lesser* General Public License because it does *Less* to protect the user's freedom than the ordinary General Public License. It also provides other free software developers Less of an advantage over competing non-free programs. These disadvantages are the reason we use the ordinary General Public License for many libraries. However, the Lesser license provides advantages in certain special circumstances.

For example, on rare occasions, there may be a special need to encourage the widest possible use of a certain library, so that it becomes a de-facto standard. To achieve this, non-free programs must be allowed to use the library. A more frequent case is that a free library does the same job as widely used non-free libraries. In this case, there is little to gain by limiting the free library to free software only, so we use the Lesser General Public License.

In other cases, permission to use a particular library in non-free programs enables a greater number of people to use a large body of free software. For example, permission to use the GNU C Library in non-free programs enables many more people to use the whole GNU operating system, as well as its variant, the GNU/Linux operating system.

Although the Lesser General Public License is Less protective of the users' freedom, it does ensure that the user of a program that is linked with the Library has the freedom and the wherewithal to run that program using a modified version of the Library.

The precise terms and conditions for copying, distribution and modification follow. Pay close attention to the difference between a "work based on the library" and a "work that uses the library". The former contains code derived from the library, whereas the latter must be combined with the library in order to run.

TERMS AND CONDITIONS FOR COPYING, DISTRIBUTION AND MODIFICATION

0. This License Agreement applies to any software library or other program which contains a notice placed by the copyright holder or other authorized party saying it may be distributed under the terms of this Lesser General Public License (also called "this License"). Each licensee is addressed as "you".

   A "library" means a collection of software functions and/or data prepared so as to be conveniently linked with application programs (which use some of those functions and data) to form executables.

The "Library", below, refers to any such software library or work which has been distributed under these terms. A "work based on the Library" means either the Library or any derivative work under copyright law: that is to say, a work containing the Library or a portion of it, either verbatim or with modifications and/or translated straightforwardly into another language. (Hereinafter, translation is included without limitation in the term "modification".)

"Source code" for a work means the preferred form of the work for making modifications to it. For a library, complete source code means all the source code for all modules it contains, plus any associated interface definition files, plus the scripts used to control compilation and installation of the library.

Activities other than copying, distribution and modification are not covered by this License; they are outside its scope. The act of running a program using the Library is not restricted, and output from such a program is covered only if its contents constitute a work based on the Library (independent of the use of the Library in a tool for writing it). Whether that is true depends on what the Library does and what the program that uses the Library does.

1. You may copy and distribute verbatim copies of the Library's complete source code as you receive it, in any medium, provided that you conspicuously and appropriately publish on each copy an appropriate copyright notice and disclaimer of warranty; keep intact all the notices that refer to this License and to the absence of any warranty; and distribute a copy of this License along with the Library.

   You may charge a fee for the physical act of transferring a copy, and you may at your option offer warranty protection in exchange for a fee.

2. You may modify your copy or copies of the Library or any portion of it, thus forming a work based on the Library, and copy and distribute such modifications or work under the terms of Section 1 above, provided that you also meet all of these conditions:

   a. The modified work must itself be a software library.

   b. You must cause the files modified to carry prominent notices stating that you changed the files and the date of any change.

   c. You must cause the whole of the work to be licensed at no charge to all third parties under the terms of this License.

   d. If a facility in the modified Library refers to a function or a table of data to be supplied by an application program that uses the facility, other than as an argument passed when the facility is invoked, then you must make a good faith effort to ensure that, in the event an application does not supply such function or table, the facility still operates, and performs whatever part of its purpose remains meaningful.

      (For example, a function in a library to compute square roots has a purpose that is entirely well-defined independent of the application. Therefore, Subsection 2d requires that any application-supplied function or table used by this function must be optional: if the application does not supply it, the square root function must still compute square roots.)

   These requirements apply to the modified work as a whole. If identifiable sections of that work are not derived from the Library, and can be reasonably considered independent and separate works in themselves, then this License, and its terms, do not apply to those sections when you distribute them as separate works. But when you distribute the same sections as part of a whole which is a work based on the Library, the distribution of the whole must be on the terms of this License, whose permissions for other licensees extend to the entire whole, and thus to each and every part regardless of who wrote it.

Thus, it is not the intent of this section to claim rights or contest your rights to work written entirely by you; rather, the intent is to exercise the right to control the distribution of derivative or collective works based on the Library.

In addition, mere aggregation of another work not based on the Library with the Library (or with a work based on the Library) on a volume of a storage or distribution medium does not bring the other work under the scope of this License.

3. You may opt to apply the terms of the ordinary GNU General Public License instead of this License to a given copy of the Library. To do this, you must alter all the notices that refer to this License, so that they refer to the ordinary GNU General Public License, version 2, instead of to this License. (If a newer version than version 2 of the ordinary GNU General Public License has appeared, then you can specify that version instead if you wish.) Do not make any other change in these notices.

Once this change is made in a given copy, it is irreversible for that copy, so the ordinary GNU General Public License applies to all subsequent copies and derivative works made from that copy.

This option is useful when you wish to copy part of the code of the Library into a program that is not a library.

4. You may copy and distribute the Library (or a portion or derivative of it, under Section 2) in object code or executable form under the terms of Sections 1 and 2 above provided that you accompany it with the complete corresponding machine-readable source code, which must be distributed under the terms of Sections 1 and 2 above on a medium customarily used for software interchange.

If distribution of object code is made by offering access to copy from a designated place, then offering equivalent access to copy the source code from the same place satisfies the requirement to distribute the source code, even though third parties are not compelled to copy the source along with the object code.

5. A program that contains no derivative of any portion of the Library, but is designed to work with the Library by being compiled or linked with it, is called a "work that uses the Library". Such a work, in isolation, is not a derivative work of the Library, and therefore falls outside the scope of this License.

However, linking a "work that uses the Library" with the Library creates an executable that is a derivative of the Library (because it contains portions of the Library), rather than a "work that uses the library". The executable is therefore covered by this License. Section 6 states terms for distribution of such executables.

When a "work that uses the Library" uses material from a header file that is part of the Library, the object code for the work may be a derivative work of the Library even though the source code is not. Whether this is true is especially significant if the work can be linked without the Library, or if the work is itself a library. The threshold for this to be true is not precisely defined by law.

If such an object file uses only numerical parameters, data structure layouts and accessors, and small macros and small inline functions (ten lines or less in length), then the use of the object file is unrestricted, regardless of whether it is legally a derivative work. (Executables containing this object code plus portions of the Library will still fall under Section 6.)

Otherwise, if the work is a derivative of the Library, you may distribute the object code for the work under the terms of Section 6. Any executables containing that work also fall under Section 6, whether or not they are linked directly with the Library itself.

6. As an exception to the Sections above, you may also combine or link a "work that uses the Library" with the Library to produce a work containing portions of the Library, and distribute that work under terms of your choice, provided that the terms permit modification of the work for the customer's own use and reverse engineering for debugging such modifications.

   You must give prominent notice with each copy of the work that the Library is used in it and that the Library and its use are covered by this License. You must supply a copy of this License. If the work during execution displays copyright notices, you must include the copyright notice for the Library among them, as well as a reference directing the user to the copy of this License. Also, you must do one of these things:

   a. Accompany the work with the complete corresponding machine-readable source code for the Library including whatever changes were used in the work (which must be distributed under Sections 1 and 2 above); and, if the work is an executable linked with the Library, with the complete machine-readable "work that uses the Library", as object code and/or source code, so that the user can modify the Library and then relink to produce a modified executable containing the modified Library. (It is understood that the user who changes the contents of definitions files in the Library will not necessarily be able to recompile the application to use the modified definitions.)

   b. Use a suitable shared library mechanism for linking with the Library. A suitable mechanism is one that (1) uses at run time a copy of the library already present on the user's computer system, rather than copying library functions into the executable, and (2) will operate properly with a modified version of the library, if the user installs one, as long as the modified version is interface-compatible with the version that the work was made with.

   c. Accompany the work with a written offer, valid for at least three years, to give the same user the materials specified in Subsection 6a, above, for a charge no more than the cost of performing this distribution.

   d. If distribution of the work is made by offering access to copy from a designated place, offer equivalent access to copy the above specified materials from the same place.

   e. Verify that the user has already received a copy of these materials or that you have already sent this user a copy.

For an executable, the required form of the "work that uses the Library" must include any data and utility programs needed for reproducing the executable from it. However, as a special exception, the materials to be distributed need not include anything that is normally distributed (in either source or binary form) with the major components (compiler, kernel, and so on) of the operating system on which the executable runs, unless that component itself accompanies the executable.

It may happen that this requirement contradicts the license restrictions of other proprietary libraries that do not normally accompany the operating system. Such a contradiction means you cannot use both them and the Library together in an executable that you distribute.

7. You may place library facilities that are a work based on the Library side-by-side in a single library together with other library facilities not covered by this License, and distribute such a combined library, provided that the separate distribution of the work based on the Library and of the other library facilities is otherwise permitted, and provided that you do these two things:

    a. Accompany the combined library with a copy of the same work based on the Library, uncombined with any other library facilities. This must be distributed under the terms of the Sections above.

    b. Give prominent notice with the combined library of the fact that part of it is a work based on the Library, and explaining where to find the accompanying uncombined form of the same work.

8. You may not copy, modify, sublicense, link with, or distribute the Library except as expressly provided under this License. Any attempt otherwise to copy, modify, sublicense, link with, or distribute the Library is void, and will automatically terminate your rights under this License. However, parties who have received copies, or rights, from you under this License will not have their licenses terminated so long as such parties remain in full compliance.

9. You are not required to accept this License, since you have not signed it. However, nothing else grants you permission to modify or distribute the Library or its derivative works. These actions are prohibited by law if you do not accept this License. Therefore, by modifying or distributing the Library (or any work based on the Library), you indicate your acceptance of this License to do so, and all its terms and conditions for copying, distributing or modifying the Library or works based on it.

10. Each time you redistribute the Library (or any work based on the Library), the recipient automatically receives a license from the original licensor to copy, distribute, link with or modify the Library subject to these terms and conditions. You may not impose any further restrictions on the recipients' exercise of the rights granted herein. You are not responsible for enforcing compliance by third parties with this License.

11. If, as a consequence of a court judgment or allegation of patent infringement or for any other reason (not limited to patent issues), conditions are imposed on you (whether by court order, agreement or otherwise) that contradict the conditions of this License, they do not excuse you from the conditions of this License. If you cannot distribute so as to satisfy simultaneously your obligations under this License and any other pertinent obligations, then as a consequence you may not distribute the Library at all. For example, if a patent license would not permit royalty-free redistribution of the Library by all those who receive copies directly or indirectly through you, then the only way you could satisfy both it and this License would be to refrain entirely from distribution of the Library.

If any portion of this section is held invalid or unenforceable under any particular circumstance, the balance of the section is intended to apply, and the section as a whole is intended to apply in other circumstances.

It is not the purpose of this section to induce you to infringe any patents or other property right claims or to contest validity of any such claims; this section has the sole purpose of protecting the integrity of the free software distribution system which is implemented by public license practices. Many people have made generous contributions to the wide range of software distributed through that system in reliance on consistent application of that system; it is up to the author/donor to decide if he or she is willing to distribute software through any other system and a licensee cannot impose that choice.

This section is intended to make thoroughly clear what is believed to be a consequence of the rest of this License.

12. If the distribution and/or use of the Library is restricted in certain countries either by patents or by copyrighted interfaces, the original copyright holder who places the Library under this License may add an explicit geographical distribution limitation excluding those countries, so that distribution is permitted only in or among countries not thus excluded. In such case, this License incorporates the limitation as if written in the body of this License.

13. The Free Software Foundation may publish revised and/or new versions of the Lesser General Public License from time to time. Such new versions will be similar in spirit to the present version, but may differ in detail to address new problems or concerns.

Each version is given a distinguishing version number. If the Library specifies a version number of this License which applies to it and "any later version", you have the option of following the terms and conditions either of that version or of any later version published by the Free Software Foundation. If the Library does not specify a license version number, you may choose any version ever published by the Free Software Foundation.

14. If you wish to incorporate parts of the Library into other free programs whose distribution conditions are incompatible with these, write to the author to ask for permission. For software which is copyrighted by the Free Software Foundation, write to the Free Software Foundation; we sometimes make exceptions for this. Our decision will be guided by the two goals of preserving the free status of all derivatives of our free software and of promoting the sharing and reuse of software generally.

NO WARRANTY

15. BECAUSE THE LIBRARY IS LICENSED FREE OF CHARGE, THERE IS NO WARRANTY FOR THE LIBRARY, TO THE EXTENT PERMITTED BY APPLICABLE LAW. EXCEPT WHEN OTHERWISE STATED IN WRITING THE COPYRIGHT HOLDERS AND/OR OTHER PARTIES PROVIDE THE LIBRARY "AS IS" WITHOUT WARRANTY OF ANY KIND, EITHER EXPRESSED OR IMPLIED, INCLUDING, BUT NOT LIMITED TO, THE IMPLIED WARRANTIES OF MERCHANTABILITY AND FITNESS FOR A PARTICULAR PURPOSE. THE ENTIRE RISK AS TO THE QUALITY AND PERFORMANCE OF THE LIBRARY IS WITH YOU. SHOULD THE LIBRARY PROVE DEFECTIVE, YOU ASSUME THE COST OF ALL NECESSARY SERVICING, REPAIR OR CORRECTION.

16. IN NO EVENT UNLESS REQUIRED BY APPLICABLE LAW OR AGREED TO IN

WRITING WILL ANY COPYRIGHT HOLDER, OR ANY OTHER PARTY WHO MAY MODIFY AND/OR REDISTRIBUTE THE LIBRARY AS PERMITTED ABOVE, BE LIABLE TO YOU FOR DAMAGES, INCLUDING ANY GENERAL, SPECIAL, INCIDENTAL OR CONSEQUENTIAL DAMAGES ARISING OUT OF THE USE OR INABILITY TO USE THE LIBRARY (INCLUDING BUT NOT LIMITED TO LOSS OF DATA OR DATA BEING RENDERED INACCURATE OR LOSSES SUSTAINED BY YOU OR THIRD PARTIES OR A FAILURE OF THE LIBRARY TO OPERATE WITH ANY OTHER SOFTWARE), EVEN IF SUCH HOLDER OR OTHER PARTY HAS BEEN ADVISED OF THE POSSIBILITY OF SUCH DAMAGES.

END OF TERMS AND CONDITIONS

How to Apply These Terms to Your New Libraries

If you develop a new library, and you want it to be of the greatest possible use to the public, we recommend making it free software that everyone can redistribute and change. You can do so by permitting redistribution under these terms (or, alternatively, under the terms of the ordinary General Public License).

To apply these terms, attach the following notices to the library. It is safest to attach them to the start of each source file to most effectively convey the exclusion of warranty; and each file should have at least the "copyright" line and a pointer to where the full notice is found.

```
one line to give the library's name and an idea of what it does.
Copyright (C) year  name of author

This library is free software; you can redistribute it and/or modify it
under the terms of the GNU Lesser General Public License as published by
the Free Software Foundation; either version 2.1 of the License, or (at
your option) any later version.

This library is distributed in the hope that it will be useful, but
WITHOUT ANY WARRANTY; without even the implied warranty of
MERCHANTABILITY or FITNESS FOR A PARTICULAR PURPOSE.  See the GNU
Lesser General Public License for more details.

You should have received a copy of the GNU Lesser General Public
License along with this library; if not, write to the Free Software
Foundation, Inc., 51 Franklin Street, Fifth Floor, Boston, MA 02110-1301,
USA.
```

Also add information on how to contact you by electronic and paper mail.

You should also get your employer (if you work as a programmer) or your school, if any, to sign a "copyright disclaimer" for the library, if necessary. Here is a sample; alter the names:

```
Yoyodyne, Inc., hereby disclaims all copyright interest in the library
'Frob' (a library for tweaking knobs) written by James Random Hacker.

signature of Ty Coon, 1 April 1990
Ty Coon, President of Vice
```

That's all there is to it!

GNU GPL with eCos Extension

Version 2, June 1991

Copyright © 1989, 1991 Free Software Foundation, Inc.

59 Temple Place – Suite 330, Boston, MA 02111-1307, USA

Preamble

The licenses for most software are designed to take away your freedom to share and change it. By contrast, the GNU General Public License is intended to guarantee your freedom to share and change free software—to make sure the software is free for all its users. This General Public License applies to most of the Free Software Foundation's software and to any other program whose authors commit to using it. (Some other Free Software Foundation software is covered by the GNU Library General Public License instead.) You can apply it to your programs, too.

When we speak of free software, we are referring to freedom, not price. Our General Public Licenses are designed to make sure that you have the freedom to distribute copies of free software (and charge for this service if you wish), that you receive source code or can get it if you want it, that you can change the software or use pieces of it in new free programs; and that you know you can do these things.

To protect your rights, we need to make restrictions that forbid anyone to deny you these rights or to ask you to surrender the rights. These restrictions translate to certain responsibilities for you if you distribute copies of the software, or if you modify it.

For example, if you distribute copies of such a program, whether gratis or for a fee, you must give the recipients all the rights that you have. You must make sure that they, too, receive or can get the source code. And you must show them these terms so they know their rights.

We protect your rights with two steps: (1) copyright the software, and (2) offer you this license which gives you legal permission to copy, distribute and/or modify the software.

Also, for each author's protection and ours, we want to make certain that everyone understands that there is no warranty for this free software. If the software is modified by someone else and passed on, we want its recipients to know that what they have is not the original, so that any problems introduced by others will not reflect on the original authors' reputations.

Finally, any free program is threatened constantly by software patents. We wish to avoid the danger that redistributors of a free program will individually obtain patent licenses, in effect making the program proprietary. To prevent this, we have made it clear that any patent must be licensed for everyone's free use or not licensed at all.

The precise terms and conditions for copying, distribution and modification follow.

TERMS AND CONDITIONS FOR COPYING, DISTRIBUTION AND MODIFICATION

1. This License applies to any program or other work which contains a notice placed by the copyright holder saying it may be distributed under the terms of this General

Public License. The "Program", below, refers to any such program or work, and a "work based on the Program" means either the Program or any derivative work under copyright law: that is to say, a work containing the Program or a portion of it, either verbatim or with modifications and/or translated into another language. (Hereinafter, translation is included without limitation in the term "modification".) Each licensee is addressed as "you".

Activities other than copying, distribution and modification are not covered by this License; they are outside its scope. The act of running the Program is not restricted, and the output from the Program is covered only if its contents constitute a work based on the Program (independent of having been made by running the Program). Whether that is true depends on what the Program does.

2. You may copy and distribute verbatim copies of the Program's source code as you receive it, in any medium, provided that you conspicuously and appropriately publish on each copy an appropriate copyright notice and disclaimer of warranty; keep intact all the notices that refer to this License and to the absence of any warranty; and give any other recipients of the Program a copy of this License along with the Program.

You may charge a fee for the physical act of transferring a copy, and you may at your option offer warranty protection in exchange for a fee.

3. You may modify your copy or copies of the Program or any portion of it, thus forming a work based on the Program, and copy and distribute such modifications or work under the terms of Section 1 above, provided that you also meet all of these conditions:

   a. You must cause the modified files to carry prominent notices stating that you changed the files and the date of any change.

   b. You must cause any work that you distribute or publish, that in whole or in part contains or is derived from the Program or any part thereof, to be licensed as a whole at no charge to all third parties under the terms of this License.

   c. If the modified program normally reads commands interactively when run, you must cause it, when started running for such interactive use in the most ordinary way, to print or display an announcement including an appropriate copyright notice and a notice that there is no warranty (or else, saying that you provide a warranty) and that users may redistribute the program under these conditions, and telling the user how to view a copy of this License. (Exception: if the Program itself is interactive but does not normally print such an announcement, your work based on the Program is not required to print an announcement.)

These requirements apply to the modified work as a whole. If identifiable sections of that work are not derived from the Program, and can be reasonably considered independent and separate works in themselves, then this License, and its terms, do not apply to those sections when you distribute them as separate works. But when you distribute the same sections as part of a whole which is a work based on the Program, the distribution of the whole must be on the terms of this License, whose permissions for other licensees extend to the entire whole, and thus to each and every part regardless of who wrote it.

Thus, it is not the intent of this section to claim rights or contest your rights to work written entirely by you; rather, the intent is to exercise the right to control the distribution of derivative or collective works based on the Program.

In addition, mere aggregation of another work not based on the Program with the Program (or with a work based on the Program) on a volume of a storage or distribution medium does not bring the other work under the scope of this License.

4. You may copy and distribute the Program (or a work based on it, under Section 2) in object code or executable form under the terms of Sections 1 and 2 above provided that you also do one of the following:

   a. Accompany it with the complete corresponding machine-readable source code, which must be distributed under the terms of Sections 1 and 2 above on a medium customarily used for software interchange; or,

   b. Accompany it with a written offer, valid for at least three years, to give any third party, for a charge no more than your cost of physically performing source distribution, a complete machine-readable copy of the corresponding source code, to be distributed under the terms of Sections 1 and 2 above on a medium customarily used for software interchange; or,

   c. Accompany it with the information you received as to the offer to distribute corresponding source code. (This alternative is allowed only for noncommercial distribution and only if you received the program in object code or executable form with such an offer, in accord with Subsection b above.)

The source code for a work means the preferred form of the work for making modifications to it. For an executable work, complete source code means all the source code for all modules it contains, plus any associated interface definition files, plus the scripts used to control compilation and installation of the executable. However, as a special exception, the source code distributed need not include anything that is normally distributed (in either source or binary form) with the major components (compiler, kernel, and so on) of the operating system on which the executable runs, unless that component itself accompanies the executable.

If distribution of executable or object code is made by offering access to copy from a designated place, then offering equivalent access to copy the source code from the same place counts as distribution of the source code, even though third parties are not compelled to copy the source along with the object code.

5. You may not copy, modify, sublicense, or distribute the Program except as expressly provided under this License. Any attempt otherwise to copy, modify, sublicense or distribute the Program is void, and will automatically terminate your rights under this License. However, parties who have received copies, or rights, from you under this License will not have their licenses terminated so long as such parties remain in full compliance.

6. You are not required to accept this License, since you have not signed it. However, nothing else grants you permission to modify or distribute the Program or its derivative works. These actions are prohibited by law if you do not accept this License. Therefore, by modifying or distributing the Program (or any work based on the Program), you indicate your acceptance of this License to do so, and all its terms and conditions for copying, distributing or modifying the Program or works based on it.

7. Each time you redistribute the Program (or any work based on the Program), the recipient automatically receives a license from the original licensor to copy, distribute or modify the Program subject to these terms and conditions. You may not impose

any further restrictions on the recipients' exercise of the rights granted herein. You are not responsible for enforcing compliance by third parties to this License.

8. If, as a consequence of a court judgment or allegation of patent infringement or for any other reason (not limited to patent issues), conditions are imposed on you (whether by court order, agreement or otherwise) that contradict the conditions of this License, they do not excuse you from the conditions of this License. If you cannot distribute so as to satisfy simultaneously your obligations under this License and any other pertinent obligations, then as a consequence you may not distribute the Program at all. For example, if a patent license would not permit royalty-free redistribution of the Program by all those who receive copies directly or indirectly through you, then the only way you could satisfy both it and this License would be to refrain entirely from distribution of the Program.

   If any portion of this section is held invalid or unenforceable under any particular circumstance, the balance of the section is intended to apply and the section as a whole is intended to apply in other circumstances.

   It is not the purpose of this section to induce you to infringe any patents or other property right claims or to contest validity of any such claims; this section has the sole purpose of protecting the integrity of the free software distribution system, which is implemented by public license practices. Many people have made generous contributions to the wide range of software distributed through that system in reliance on consistent application of that system; it is up to the author/donor to decide if he or she is willing to distribute software through any other system and a licensee cannot impose that choice.

   This section is intended to make thoroughly clear what is believed to be a consequence of the rest of this License.

9. If the distribution and/or use of the Program is restricted in certain countries either by patents or by copyrighted interfaces, the original copyright holder who places the Program under this License may add an explicit geographical distribution limitation excluding those countries, so that distribution is permitted only in or among countries not thus excluded. In such case, this License incorporates the limitation as if written in the body of this License.

10. The Free Software Foundation may publish revised and/or new versions of the General Public License from time to time. Such new versions will be similar in spirit to the present version, but may differ in detail to address new problems or concerns.

   Each version is given a distinguishing version number. If the Program specifies a version number of this License which applies to it and "any later version", you have the option of following the terms and conditions either of that version or of any later version published by the Free Software Foundation. If the Program does not specify a version number of this License, you may choose any version ever published by the Free Software Foundation.

11. If you wish to incorporate parts of the Program into other free programs whose distribution conditions are different, write to the author to ask for permission. For software which is copyrighted by the Free Software Foundation, write to the Free Software Foundation; we sometimes make exceptions for this. Our decision will be guided by the two

goals of preserving the free status of all derivatives of our free software and of promoting the sharing and reuse of software generally.

NO WARRANTY

12. BECAUSE THE PROGRAM IS LICENSED FREE OF CHARGE, THERE IS NO WARRANTY FOR THE PROGRAM, TO THE EXTENT PERMITTED BY APPLICABLE LAW. EXCEPT WHEN OTHERWISE STATED IN WRITING THE COPYRIGHT HOLDERS AND/OR OTHER PARTIES PROVIDE THE PROGRAM "AS IS" WITHOUT WARRANTY OF ANY KIND, EITHER EXPRESSED OR IMPLIED, INCLUDING, BUT NOT LIMITED TO, THE IMPLIED WARRANTIES OF MERCHANTABILITY AND FITNESS FOR A PARTICULAR PURPOSE. THE ENTIRE RISK AS TO THE QUALITY AND PERFORMANCE OF THE PROGRAM IS WITH YOU. SHOULD THE PROGRAM PROVE DEFECTIVE, YOU ASSUME THE COST OF ALL NECESSARY SERVICING, REPAIR OR CORRECTION.

13. IN NO EVENT UNLESS REQUIRED BY APPLICABLE LAW OR AGREED TO IN WRITING WILL ANY COPYRIGHT HOLDER, OR ANY OTHER PARTY WHO MAY MODIFY AND/OR REDISTRIBUTE THE PROGRAM AS PERMITTED ABOVE, BE LIABLE TO YOU FOR DAMAGES, INCLUDING ANY GENERAL, SPECIAL, INCIDENTAL OR CONSEQUENTIAL DAMAGES ARISING OUT OF THE USE OR INABILITY TO USE THE PROGRAM (INCLUDING BUT NOT LIMITED TO LOSS OF DATA OR DATA BEING RENDERED INACCURATE OR LOSSES SUSTAINED BY YOU OR THIRD PARTIES OR A FAILURE OF THE PROGRAM TO OPERATE WITH ANY OTHER PROGRAMS), EVEN IF SUCH HOLDER OR OTHER PARTY HAS BEEN ADVISED OF THE POSSIBILITY OF SUCH DAMAGES.

ECOS EXTENSION

14. As a special exception, if other files instantiate templates or use macros or inline functions from this file, or you compile this file and link it with other works to produce a work based on this file, this file does not by itself cause the resulting work to be covered by the GNU General Public License. However the source code for this file must still be made available in accordance with section (3) of the GNU General Public License v2.

This exception does not invalidate any other reasons why a work based on this file might be covered by the GNU General Public License.

END OF TERMS AND CONDITIONS

How to Apply These Terms to Your New Programs

If you develop a new program, and you want it to be of the greatest possible use to the public, the best way to achieve this is to make it free software which everyone can redistribute and change under these terms.

To do so, attach the following notices to the program. It is safest to attach them to the start of each source file to most effectively convey the exclusion of warranty; and each file should have at least the "copyright" line and a pointer to where the full notice is found.

```
one line to give the program's name and an idea of what it does.
Copyright (C) 19yy  name of author

This program is free software; you can redistribute it and/or
modify it under the terms of the GNU General Public License
as published by the Free Software Foundation; either version 2
of the License, or (at your option) any later version.

This program is distributed in the hope that it will be useful,
but WITHOUT ANY WARRANTY; without even the implied warranty of
MERCHANTABILITY or FITNESS FOR A PARTICULAR PURPOSE.  See the
GNU General Public License for more details.

You should have received a copy of the GNU General Public License along
with this program; if not, write to the Free Software Foundation, Inc.,
59 Temple Place, Suite 330, Boston, MA 02111-1307, USA.
```

Also add information on how to contact you by electronic and paper mail.

If the program is interactive, make it output a short notice like this when it starts in an interactive mode:

```
Gnomovision version 69, Copyright (C) 19yy name of author
Gnomovision comes with ABSOLUTELY NO WARRANTY; for details
type 'show w'.  This is free software, and you are welcome
to redistribute it under certain conditions; type 'show c'
for details.
```

The hypothetical commands 'show w' and 'show c' should show the appropriate parts of the General Public License. Of course, the commands you use may be called something other than 'show w' and 'show c'; they could even be mouse-clicks or menu items—whatever suits your program.

You should also get your employer (if you work as a programmer) or your school, if any, to sign a "copyright disclaimer" for the program, if necessary. Here is a sample; alter the names:

```
Yoyodyne, Inc., hereby disclaims all copyright
interest in the program 'Gnomovision'
(which makes passes at compilers) written
by James Hacker.

signature of Ty Coon, 1 April 1989
Ty Coon, President of Vice
```

This General Public License does not permit incorporating your program into proprietary programs. If your program is a subroutine library, you may consider it more useful to permit linking proprietary applications with the library. If this is what you want to do, use the GNU Library General Public License instead of this License.

GNU-FDL

Version 1.3, 3 November 2008

Copyright © 2000, 2001, 2002, 2007, 2008 Free Software Foundation, Inc.
`http://fsf.org/`

Everyone is permitted to copy and distribute verbatim copies
of this license document, but changing it is not allowed.

0. PREAMBLE

The purpose of this License is to make a manual, textbook, or other functional and useful document *free* in the sense of freedom: to assure everyone the effective freedom to copy and redistribute it, with or without modifying it, either commercially or non-commercially. Secondarily, this License preserves for the author and publisher a way to get credit for their work, while not being considered responsible for modifications made by others.

This License is a kind of "copyleft", which means that derivative works of the document must themselves be free in the same sense. It complements the GNU General Public License, which is a copyleft license designed for free software.

We have designed this License in order to use it for manuals for free software, because free software needs free documentation: a free program should come with manuals providing the same freedoms that the software does. But this License is not limited to software manuals; it can be used for any textual work, regardless of subject matter or whether it is published as a printed book. We recommend this License principally for works whose purpose is instruction or reference.

1. APPLICABILITY AND DEFINITIONS

This License applies to any manual or other work, in any medium, that contains a notice placed by the copyright holder saying it can be distributed under the terms of this License. Such a notice grants a world-wide, royalty-free license, unlimited in duration, to use that work under the conditions stated herein. The "Document", below, refers to any such manual or work. Any member of the public is a licensee, and is addressed as "you". You accept the license if you copy, modify or distribute the work in a way requiring permission under copyright law.

A "Modified Version" of the Document means any work containing the Document or a portion of it, either copied verbatim, or with modifications and/or translated into another language.

A "Secondary Section" is a named appendix or a front-matter section of the Document that deals exclusively with the relationship of the publishers or authors of the Document to the Document's overall subject (or to related matters) and contains nothing that could fall directly within that overall subject. (Thus, if the Document is in part a textbook of mathematics, a Secondary Section may not explain any mathematics.) The relationship could be a matter of historical connection with the subject or with related matters, or of legal, commercial, philosophical, ethical or political position regarding them.

The "Invariant Sections" are certain Secondary Sections whose titles are designated, as being those of Invariant Sections, in the notice that says that the Document is released under this License. If a section does not fit the above definition of Secondary then it is not allowed to be designated as Invariant. The Document may contain zero Invariant Sections. If the Document does not identify any Invariant Sections then there are none.

The "Cover Texts" are certain short passages of text that are listed, as Front-Cover Texts or Back-Cover Texts, in the notice that says that the Document is released under this License. A Front-Cover Text may be at most 5 words, and a Back-Cover Text may be at most 25 words.

A "Transparent" copy of the Document means a machine-readable copy, represented in a format whose specification is available to the general public, that is suitable for revising the document straightforwardly with generic text editors or (for images composed of pixels) generic paint programs or (for drawings) some widely available drawing editor, and that is suitable for input to text formatters or for automatic translation to a variety of formats suitable for input to text formatters. A copy made in an otherwise Transparent file format whose markup, or absence of markup, has been arranged to thwart or discourage subsequent modification by readers is not Transparent. An image format is not Transparent if used for any substantial amount of text. A copy that is not "Transparent" is called "Opaque".

Examples of suitable formats for Transparent copies include plain ASCII without markup, Texinfo input format, LaTeX input format, SGML or XML using a publicly available DTD, and standard-conforming simple HTML, PostScript or PDF designed for human modification. Examples of transparent image formats include PNG, XCF and JPG. Opaque formats include proprietary formats that can be read and edited only by proprietary word processors, SGML or XML for which the DTD and/or processing tools are not generally available, and the machine-generated HTML, PostScript or PDF produced by some word processors for output purposes only.

The "Title Page" means, for a printed book, the title page itself, plus such following pages as are needed to hold, legibly, the material this License requires to appear in the title page. For works in formats which do not have any title page as such, "Title Page" means the text near the most prominent appearance of the work's title, preceding the beginning of the body of the text.

The "publisher" means any person or entity that distributes copies of the Document to the public.

A section "Entitled XYZ" means a named subunit of the Document whose title either is precisely XYZ or contains XYZ in parentheses following text that translates XYZ in another language. (Here XYZ stands for a specific section name mentioned below, such as "Acknowledgements", "Dedications", "Endorsements", or "History".) To "Preserve the Title" of such a section when you modify the Document means that it remains a section "Entitled XYZ" according to this definition.

The Document may include Warranty Disclaimers next to the notice which states that this License applies to the Document. These Warranty Disclaimers are considered to be included by reference in this License, but only as regards disclaiming warranties: any other implication that these Warranty Disclaimers may have is void and has no effect on the meaning of this License.

2. VERBATIM COPYING

You may copy and distribute the Document in any medium, either commercially or noncommercially, provided that this License, the copyright notices, and the license notice saying this License applies to the Document are reproduced in all copies, and that you add no other conditions whatsoever to those of this License. You may not use technical measures to obstruct or control the reading or further copying of the copies you make or distribute. However, you may accept compensation in exchange for copies. If you distribute a large enough number of copies you must also follow the conditions in section 3.

You may also lend copies, under the same conditions stated above, and you may publicly display copies.

3. COPYING IN QUANTITY

If you publish printed copies (or copies in media that commonly have printed covers) of the Document, numbering more than 100, and the Document's license notice requires Cover Texts, you must enclose the copies in covers that carry, clearly and legibly, all these Cover Texts: Front-Cover Texts on the front cover, and Back-Cover Texts on the back cover. Both covers must also clearly and legibly identify you as the publisher of these copies. The front cover must present the full title with all words of the title equally prominent and visible. You may add other material on the covers in addition. Copying with changes limited to the covers, as long as they preserve the title of the Document and satisfy these conditions, can be treated as verbatim copying in other respects.

If the required texts for either cover are too voluminous to fit legibly, you should put the first ones listed (as many as fit reasonably) on the actual cover, and continue the rest onto adjacent pages.

If you publish or distribute Opaque copies of the Document numbering more than 100, you must either include a machine-readable Transparent copy along with each Opaque copy, or state in or with each Opaque copy a computer-network location from which the general network-using public has access to download using public-standard network protocols a complete Transparent copy of the Document, free of added material. If you use the latter option, you must take reasonably prudent steps, when you begin distribution of Opaque copies in quantity, to ensure that this Transparent copy will remain thus accessible at the stated location until at least one year after the last time you distribute an Opaque copy (directly or through your agents or retailers) of that edition to the public.

It is requested, but not required, that you contact the authors of the Document well before redistributing any large number of copies, to give them a chance to provide you with an updated version of the Document.

4. MODIFICATIONS

You may copy and distribute a Modified Version of the Document under the conditions of sections 2 and 3 above, provided that you release the Modified Version under precisely this License, with the Modified Version filling the role of the Document, thus licensing distribution and modification of the Modified Version to whoever possesses a copy of it. In addition, you must do these things in the Modified Version:

A. Use in the Title Page (and on the covers, if any) a title distinct from that of the Document, and from those of previous versions (which should, if there were any, be listed in the History section of the Document). You may use the same title as a previous version if the original publisher of that version gives permission.

B. List on the Title Page, as authors, one or more persons or entities responsible for authorship of the modifications in the Modified Version, together with at least five of the principal authors of the Document (all of its principal authors, if it has fewer than five), unless they release you from this requirement.

C. State on the Title page the name of the publisher of the Modified Version, as the publisher.

D. Preserve all the copyright notices of the Document.

E. Add an appropriate copyright notice for your modifications adjacent to the other copyright notices.

F. Include, immediately after the copyright notices, a license notice giving the public permission to use the Modified Version under the terms of this License, in the form shown in the Addendum below.

G. Preserve in that license notice the full lists of Invariant Sections and required Cover Texts given in the Document's license notice.

H. Include an unaltered copy of this License.

I. Preserve the section Entitled "History", Preserve its Title, and add to it an item stating at least the title, year, new authors, and publisher of the Modified Version as given on the Title Page. If there is no section Entitled "History" in the Document, create one stating the title, year, authors, and publisher of the Document as given on its Title Page, then add an item describing the Modified Version as stated in the previous sentence.

J. Preserve the network location, if any, given in the Document for public access to a Transparent copy of the Document, and likewise the network locations given in the Document for previous versions it was based on. These may be placed in the "History" section. You may omit a network location for a work that was published at least four years before the Document itself, or if the original publisher of the version it refers to gives permission.

K. For any section Entitled "Acknowledgements" or "Dedications", Preserve the Title of the section, and preserve in the section all the substance and tone of each of the contributor acknowledgements and/or dedications given therein.

L. Preserve all the Invariant Sections of the Document, unaltered in their text and in their titles. Section numbers or the equivalent are not considered part of the section titles.

M. Delete any section Entitled "Endorsements". Such a section may not be included in the Modified Version.

N. Do not retitle any existing section to be Entitled "Endorsements" or to conflict in title with any Invariant Section.

O. Preserve any Warranty Disclaimers.

If the Modified Version includes new front-matter sections or appendices that qualify as Secondary Sections and contain no material copied from the Document, you may at your option designate some or all of these sections as invariant. To do this, add their titles to the list of Invariant Sections in the Modified Version's license notice. These titles must be distinct from any other section titles.

You may add a section Entitled "Endorsements", provided it contains nothing but endorsements of your Modified Version by various parties—for example, statements of peer review or that the text has been approved by an organization as the authoritative definition of a standard.

You may add a passage of up to five words as a Front-Cover Text, and a passage of up to 25 words as a Back-Cover Text, to the end of the list of Cover Texts in the Modified Version. Only one passage of Front-Cover Text and one of Back-Cover Text may be added by (or through arrangements made by) any one entity. If the Document already includes a cover text for the same cover, previously added by you or by arrangement made by the same entity you are acting on behalf of, you may not add another; but you may replace the old one, on explicit permission from the previous publisher that added the old one.

The author(s) and publisher(s) of the Document do not by this License give permission to use their names for publicity for or to assert or imply endorsement of any Modified Version.

5. COMBINING DOCUMENTS

You may combine the Document with other documents released under this License, under the terms defined in section 4 above for modified versions, provided that you include in the combination all of the Invariant Sections of all of the original documents, unmodified, and list them all as Invariant Sections of your combined work in its license notice, and that you preserve all their Warranty Disclaimers.

The combined work need only contain one copy of this License, and multiple identical Invariant Sections may be replaced with a single copy. If there are multiple Invariant Sections with the same name but different contents, make the title of each such section unique by adding at the end of it, in parentheses, the name of the original author or publisher of that section if known, or else a unique number. Make the same adjustment to the section titles in the list of Invariant Sections in the license notice of the combined work.

In the combination, you must combine any sections Entitled "History" in the various original documents, forming one section Entitled "History"; likewise combine any sections Entitled "Acknowledgements", and any sections Entitled "Dedications". You must delete all sections Entitled "Endorsements."

6. COLLECTIONS OF DOCUMENTS

You may make a collection consisting of the Document and other documents released under this License, and replace the individual copies of this License in the various documents with a single copy that is included in the collection, provided that you follow the rules of this License for verbatim copying of each of the documents in all other respects.

You may extract a single document from such a collection, and distribute it individually under this License, provided you insert a copy of this License into the extracted document, and follow this License in all other respects regarding verbatim copying of that document.

7. AGGREGATION WITH INDEPENDENT WORKS

A compilation of the Document or its derivatives with other separate and independent documents or works, in or on a volume of a storage or distribution medium, is called an "aggregate" if the copyright resulting from the compilation is not used to limit the legal rights of the compilation's users beyond what the individual works permit. When the Document is included in an aggregate, this License does not apply to the other works in the aggregate which are not themselves derivative works of the Document.

If the Cover Text requirement of section 3 is applicable to these copies of the Document, then if the Document is less than one half of the entire aggregate, the Document's Cover Texts may be placed on covers that bracket the Document within the aggregate, or the electronic equivalent of covers if the Document is in electronic form. Otherwise they must appear on printed covers that bracket the whole aggregate.

8. TRANSLATION

Translation is considered a kind of modification, so you may distribute translations of the Document under the terms of section 4. Replacing Invariant Sections with translations requires special permission from their copyright holders, but you may include translations of some or all Invariant Sections in addition to the original versions of these Invariant Sections. You may include a translation of this License, and all the license notices in the Document, and any Warranty Disclaimers, provided that you also include the original English version of this License and the original versions of those notices and disclaimers. In case of a disagreement between the translation and the original version of this License or a notice or disclaimer, the original version will prevail.

If a section in the Document is Entitled "Acknowledgements", "Dedications", or "History", the requirement (section 4) to Preserve its Title (section 1) will typically require changing the actual title.

9. TERMINATION

You may not copy, modify, sublicense, or distribute the Document except as expressly provided under this License. Any attempt otherwise to copy, modify, sublicense, or distribute it is void, and will automatically terminate your rights under this License.

However, if you cease all violation of this License, then your license from a particular copyright holder is reinstated (a) provisionally, unless and until the copyright holder explicitly and finally terminates your license, and (b) permanently, if the copyright holder fails to notify you of the violation by some reasonable means prior to 60 days after the cessation.

Moreover, your license from a particular copyright holder is reinstated permanently if the copyright holder notifies you of the violation by some reasonable means, this is the first time you have received notice of violation of this License (for any work) from that copyright holder, and you cure the violation prior to 30 days after your receipt of the notice.

Termination of your rights under this section does not terminate the licenses of parties who have received copies or rights from you under this License. If your rights have been terminated and not permanently reinstated, receipt of a copy of some or all of the same material does not give you any rights to use it.

10. FUTURE REVISIONS OF THIS LICENSE

The Free Software Foundation may publish new, revised versions of the GNU Free Documentation License from time to time. Such new versions will be similar in spirit to the present version, but may differ in detail to address new problems or concerns. See http://www.gnu.org/copyleft/.

Each version of the License is given a distinguishing version number. If the Document specifies that a particular numbered version of this License "or any later version" applies to it, you have the option of following the terms and conditions either of that specified version or of any later version that has been published (not as a draft) by the Free Software Foundation. If the Document does not specify a version number of this License, you may choose any version ever published (not as a draft) by the Free Software Foundation. If the Document specifies that a proxy can decide which future versions of this License can be used, that proxy's public statement of acceptance of a version permanently authorizes you to choose that version for the Document.

11. RELICENSING

"Massive Multiauthor Collaboration Site" (or "MMC Site") means any World Wide Web server that publishes copyrightable works and also provides prominent facilities for anybody to edit those works. A public wiki that anybody can edit is an example of such a server. A "Massive Multiauthor Collaboration" (or "MMC") contained in the site means any set of copyrightable works thus published on the MMC site.

"CC-BY-SA" means the Creative Commons Attribution-Share Alike 3.0 license published by Creative Commons Corporation, a not-for-profit corporation with a principal place of business in San Francisco, California, as well as future copyleft versions of that license published by that same organization.

"Incorporate" means to publish or republish a Document, in whole or in part, as part of another Document.

An MMC is "eligible for relicensing" if it is licensed under this License, and if all works that were first published under this License somewhere other than this MMC, and subsequently incorporated in whole or in part into the MMC, (1) had no cover texts or invariant sections, and (2) were thus incorporated prior to November 1, 2008.

The operator of an MMC Site may republish an MMC contained in the site under CC-BY-SA on the same site at any time before August 1, 2009, provided the MMC is eligible for relicensing.

ADDENDUM: How to use this License for your documents

To use this License in a document you have written, include a copy of the License in the document and put the following copyright and license notices just after the title page:

```
Copyright (C)  year  your name.
Permission is granted to copy, distribute and/or modify this document
under the terms of the GNU Free Documentation License, Version 1.3
or any later version published by the Free Software Foundation;
with no Invariant Sections, no Front-Cover Texts, and no Back-Cover
Texts.  A copy of the license is included in the section entitled ''GNU
Free Documentation License''.
```

If you have Invariant Sections, Front-Cover Texts and Back-Cover Texts, replace the "with...Texts." line with this:

```
with the Invariant Sections being list their titles, with
the Front-Cover Texts being list, and with the Back-Cover Texts
being list.
```

If you have Invariant Sections without Cover Texts, or some other combination of the three, merge those two alternatives to suit the situation.

If your document contains nontrivial examples of program code, we recommend releasing these examples in parallel under your choice of free software license, such as the GNU General Public License, to permit their use in free software.

Concept Index

Function and Data Index

Type Index

www.ingramcontent.com/pod-product-compliance
Lightning Source LLC
LaVergne TN
LVHW060147070326

832902LV00018B/2998